Farmhouse Kitchen

Farmhouse Kitchen

In conjunction with the Yorkshire Television Series

by Audrey Ellis

With drawings by Kate Simunek

STANLEY PAUL/LONDON

STANLEY PAUL & CO LTD
178–202 Great Portland Street, London W1

AN IMPRINT OF THE HUTCHINSON GROUP

London Melbourne Sydney
Auckland Johannesburg Cape Town
and agencies throughout the world

First published 1971

*This book has been set in Imprint type, printed in Great Britain
on antique wove paper by Anchor Press, and
bound by Wm. Brendon, both of Tiptree, Essex*

ISBN 0 09 107640 4 (cased)
0 09 107641 2 (paper)

Contents

Introduction

The farmhouse kitchens of my childhood were warm, welcoming places. I remember them with love, for there I first learned to enjoy cooking.

For me, the country was heaven. I was born a town child, in the elegant Georgian house near Kensington Gardens, where Barrie's magic pen had conjured up Peter Pan and Wendy. My brother and I did not much enjoy playing in the prim, paved back garden of Leinster Corner House. We preferred to climb up the rickety outside staircase at the end, leading to Barrie's old study over the stables; empty then except for his writing chair and desk, which became in turn pirate ship, Indian fort, and Crusader's castle.

Every fine day we spent some hours in Kensington Gardens, where at least there was grass and space to run about. We dutifully bowled hoops along the neat paths bordered by low iron railings, sailed boats on the Round Pond, and gathered conkers under the majestic trees of the Broad Walk. But our hearts were in the country.

We were fortunate in having an indulgent, hospitable country parson for an uncle. He married rather late in life, a delightful woman, and these dear people were childless.

So we were always welcome to visit them, peaky after measles or mumps, or during the holidays. Our parents preferred town life but firmly believed in country air for children. We spent a great deal of time with these kind relatives, first at the Vicarage in a pretty Sussex village, Ifield; and later at Maidwell Rectory near Northampton.

I remember perfectly the Vicarage garden, the lawns mowed in alternate matt and shiny strips, the strawberries and raspberries and Victoria plums you could pick yourself and eat, warm from the sun, if the gardener said you might. I remember the Vicarage cow's incredible eyelashes, the excitement of seeing her being milked and the butter churned; and if more cream was needed we only had to fetch it from a neighbouring farm. Almost every day we made an excuse to go there. We always went round through

7

the yard, straight to the kitchen door, my brother running ahead whooping to frighten the hens.

Perhaps it is a composite memory of the many farmhouse kitchens I knew in my childhood, but I seem to see that room now in my mind's eye, wonderfully distinct and clear.

The door is always ajar, partly because visitors are so often in and out, and partly to let in more light. The tiny windows are set in deep recesses, painted Windsor brown. Titanic potted geraniums crowd the sills, jostling for space with the china tobacco jar, a wooden biscuit barrel with a polished silver handle, and a formidable spike impaling recipes, bills, and reminders such as *Do church flowers Saturday*.

The walls are whitewashed, with odd, inexplicable beams here and there. The floor, made of grey stone flags, dips a little near the door. It is scattered with braided rag rugs which have faded from brash red and green to subtle pinky grey and lichen colours.

At one end there is a vast kitchen range, replete with ovens for roasting, baking and warming. The hob is never empty. A pot-bellied black kettle is always just on the boil, and something is eternally simmering in a deep oval cast-iron casserole with a massive handle.

Wooden tables occupy the centre of the floor, scrubbed and sanded to a silvery sheen. There are chairs to match, with seats comfortably carved to the shape of the human form. In front of the range there is a shallow basket with a dilapidated cushion. Sometimes it is empty, sometimes occupied by the kitchen cat and a litter of kittens, or a sorrowful Sealyham with an injured paw.

There is also a ladder-backed rocking chair with a mending basket full of neatly paired socks on the seat, seeming to reserve it for the next industrious person prepared to sit down and get on with the work.

A dresser of noble proportions almost covers one wall. Serving dishes and dinner plates of a size fit for turkey, capon and sirloin are propped up on ledges. The pattern is elaborate but homely, plum red on white. Saucers and teaplates are piled on that dresser, seemingly by the dozen. An army of breakfast cups hangs temptingly above. There is always a squat Toby jug of cream, covered with a circle of muslin weighted down with blue glass beads against the intrusion of flies, or kitchen cat's inquisitive paw. Sometimes there is a big crock of eggs, still smeared and befeathered, just collected and waiting to be washed.

In a corner, a very shallow sink, biscuit coloured without and white within, is served by a brass tap placed mysteriously high on the wall, and flanked by a cage-like wooden plate rack full of shiny saucepan lids.

There is a larder large enough to walk into, with wooden shelves and marble and slate shelves; a white-washed window, a meat safe, stone jars and vegetable sacks on the floor. A place of shadows and mysteries, with a candle end and matches ready near the door in case a real search is needed. There is also a pantry stocked with row upon row of bottled fruit and jam, jellies, syrups, relishes, pickles and chutneys.

The stove never goes out, so that kitchen is always warm and always full of pleasant sounds. The flies buzz lazily, the cat purrs, or a dog snuffles in its sleep. The kettle sings very softly, and the wall clock, which is encased in dark wood and has a good deal of brass about it, ticks comfortably. Glorious smells arise, and mingle. Smells of bacon frying, bread baking, jam boiling, beef roasting.

Here I first felt the glorious satisfaction of punching my small fist deep into the satiny surface of newly risen dough, and here I first knocked up the edge of a pastry pie, decorated with diamond-shaped leaves I had cut out myself. I was never allowed near the kitchen in London, but this was the country, so it was different. My brother prodded pigs in the yard and squealed with them, while the farmer's wife gave me my first lessons in cooking. We were both perfectly happy.

Many splendid dishes came from those old farmhouse kitchens. Crisp Yorkshire puddings, eaten with gravy before the Sunday joint was served. Succulent hams, salted and smoked in the inglenook, then baked in a flour-and-water crust to conserve all the goodness. Cakes, light and feathery with dozens of eggs, or rich and solid, encrusted with the jewelled gleam of dried fruit. Jams that smelt of summer itself. Bottled fruit winking richer and larger than life through the glass, put up specially for the local Show. Pasties and pikelets, tea breads and buns—the list is endless.

In those days, farmhouses were remote from shops. To provide a varied menu all round the year, a farmer's wife had to use and preserve the food to hand in many different ways, especially the fruit and vegetables growing conveniently close to the kitchen door. When a pig was killed, every bit was eaten in some form or other, except the squeal!

The farmhouse kitchen of today has changed a little. The old sink has gone, and some modern units have been installed, looking somewhat insignificant and lost in the unaccustomed vastness of their setting. The tables, perhaps, have been topped with Formica, and where the old dresser stood a chest freezer now extends, clinically severe, against the wall.

Instead of good, old-fashioned baker's yeast, wines are made with a yeast chosen to impart the character of a sophisticated Pommard or even Champagne. Vegetables are bottled in a pressure cooker, instead of by the risky old water-bath method, or possibly even frozen instead. These modern aids make life a little easier, of course.

But the grand old tradition of cooking goes on. Strangely enough, the country arts which suffered a decline in the years between the wars, enjoyed a tremendous renaissance in the early forties. Bottling and jamming and preserving of all kinds were patriotic and important. Home brewed beers, and wines, made it easy to bear the shortages at the local. And if, when necessity prodded no longer, enthusiasm might have waned, a new generation was growing up which found it *fun* to preserve, bake and brew. Breadmaking has almost become a fashion with young country housewives, for instance. Most of them are adepts in the art of freezing every likely and unlikely food, with surprising success.

And the turn of the seasons still goes on. New potatoes are buried in sand on Midsummer Day, to reappear at Christmas. Blackcurrants are made into jam and jelly, French beans are packed in salt, green walnuts pricked and pickled, tomatoes made into chutney, and parsnips into wine. Then it is soon time for the first early potatoes again.

This is not intended to be a comprehensive recipe book. It is intended rather to give information and instruction in the less well known but fascinating crafts of the rural housewife. Some may be possible for you to copy, some may not, but no process described is difficult. Farmhouse cookery has never been elaborate though it may take time. It is always simple, always superb.

You need only follow the directions, to discover many of the delights farming families have enjoyed for centuries, and still enjoy today, up and down the country.

AUDREY ELLIS

Some useful facts and figures

Below is a table giving equivalent Gas Mark, Fahrenheit and Centigrade oven temperatures for most cookers.

OVEN TEMPERATURE CHART

Description	Gas mark	°Fahrenheit	°Centigrade
Very cool	Low	200	100
Very cool	$\frac{1}{4}$	225	110
Cool	$\frac{1}{2}$	250	120
Very slow	1	275	135
Very slow	2	300	150
Slow	3	325	165
Moderate	4	350	180
Moderately hot	5	375	190
Moderately hot	6	400	205
Hot	7	425	220
Very hot	8	450	230
Extremely hot	9	475	240

Note: This chart is only a guide and all cookers vary, so it is important to follow the manufacturer's instructions for your particular cooker, particularly if it is of a new type.

Solid fuel cookers: Many people, especially those in the country, have solid fuel cookers and it is extremely difficult to give baking directions for these as different makes vary enormously. It is therefore most important to follow the manufacturer's instructions regarding oven temperatures and as a guide follow the Fahrenheit temperature given. Those with solid fuel cookers may find it worth while investing in an oven thermometer which can be purchased quite cheaply from many large stores throughout the country, so that they are able to tell the temperature of their ovens at any given time.

Metrication

With the advent of metrication in the near future it is a good idea to understand the principles involved.

At the time of writing it is generally agreed that we should use 25 grammes to the ounce as the nearest easily workable figure instead of the exact conversion of 28·35 grammes for solid measures; and 500 millilitres to the pint, the exact conversion being 568 millilitres. As both these measures are slightly less than the exact conversion it ensures that solid and liquid measures are kept in proportion. This has been proved by experiment to be a most satisfactory method, e.g. the basic ingredients for white sauce:

White sauce:	*Imperial*	*Metric:*
	1 oz. butter	25 g. butter
	1 oz. flour	25 g. flour
	½ pint milk	250 ml. milk

Oven temperatures will be given in °Celsius (on which the Centigrade system is based), and conversions will be rounded off to give a convenient equivalent to °Fahrenheit.

°Fahrenheit	Approx. °Celsius	°Fahrenheit	Approx. °Celsius
225	105	350	175
250	120	375	190
275	135	400	205
300	150	425	220
325	165	450	230

Sizes of pans:
6 inch–15 cm., 7 inch–17·5 cm., 8 inch–20 cm., 9 inch–22·5 cm.
Note: Adjusting the quantities of seasonings, spices and flavourings to a converted recipe has been found to present no problems, if scant measures are used. Where eggs are included in the recipe, a better conversion will be made if small eggs are used rather than large, or if the quantities are considerable, by using one egg less, or three large eggs rather than four of medium size.

General measures: Unless otherwise stated, throughout this book all spoon measures are taken as level.

3 teaspoons—1 tablespoon   1 British Imperial pint—20 fl.oz
8 tablespoons—¼ pint   1 British Imperial cup—10 fl.oz.
(½ pint)

Wine-making, beer and other drinks

This country possesses an abundance of fruits, flowers, vegetables, herbs and cereals from which palatable and sometimes extremely potent drinks can be fermented. I have good reason to know this, because I was once invited to taste a number of farmhouse wines which my hostess considered had just reached perfection. After a polite sip from several tiny glasses, and a few second pourings to help give a considered opinion, I began to find the kitchen rather warm and my head rather swimmy. Deciding to leave before worse befell, I bent down to retrieve my muddy Wellingtons from beside the stove, subsided among a welter of other people's boots and some angry Jack Russell terriers, and fell sound asleep.

The gin palaces of the eighteenth century used to display signs, 'Drunk for a penny, dead drunk for twopence, clean straw free'. My hostess kindly made no charge for tucking me up on a sofa to sleep it off, and I didn't even pay a well merited twopence. But the experience gave me a healthy respect for the potency of home-made wines.

Wine-making is one of the oldest domestic arts, frequently referred to in the Bible. As early as A.D. 200, rich people in England were drinking wine imported from the Continent, while farmers drank home-made beer brewed from wheat and honey. After the Romans left, Britain was invaded by the hard-drinking Angles and Saxons. Their specialities were mead and ale. Mead was reserved for festive occasions, and the origin of our 'honey-moon' dates from the days of riotous mead-drinking parties which went on for four weeks after a wedding. During the middle ages, farmers drank home-made ale, mead and cider, and as sugar was becoming less scarce and expensive, they began to make their own wines. A book published in England in 1568 prescribes such wines for many ailments, and by the seventeenth century most manor houses and large farms had their own still rooms.

Mrs. Beeton's first *Cookery and Household Management* book came out in 1861, and among this wide and varied collection of recipes there are a number for making wine. Wine-making was not so much a hobby as part of the domestic chores of the day, that included jam-making, cake baking, etc. However, the quality varied; for it was the habit to use ale or bread yeast spread on toast and float it on the must. The main disadvantage of this method was the danger from infection since such a large surface of the wine was exposed to the air.

Another disadvantage is that the yeast will multiply rapidly but without working on the must to any great extent. The result was often a sweet wine with a low alcohol content, and brandy was added to remedy the deficiency.

The habit of making wine at home almost died out between 1885 and 1945, but it has now returned, and to the traditions of the past we can add improved methods based on scientific know-ledge and go ahead with confidence to produce wines of surprising quality. The methods are simple, but they *must* be observed. A common failing is impatience. So many people expect immediate results and consequently offer 'wine' that is still fermenting, has not yet cleared to brilliance, or has simply not finished maturing. As you learn more about the processes of wine-making, you will realise that it cannot possibly be ready for drinking until all the essential changes have taken place. So, you will leave it alone quietly to mature in the dark, and when the right time comes you will congratulate yourself on your wisdom.

Wine-maker's vocabulary

Before proceeding farther, there are various words which will keep appearing in recipes and which require some explanation.

Acid: Where no acid is present in the vegetables or flowers used, citrus fruits can remedy this: oranges, lemons, grapefruit. These also improve the flavour subtly, e.g. the bitterness of grapefruit. However, citric acid crystals may be used instead allowing a teaspoonful per lemon.

Body: The fullness of wine.

Campden tablets: Useful in wine-making for various sterilization or purification purposes. It is well worth adding these to sterilize the must as a matter of habit. Crush one tablet per gallon and add the crystals to the must when cool, so that the sulphur dioxide given off can kill any wild yeasts and bacteria that may be present. Add yeast 24 hours later.

Dry: A wine is said to be dry when all the sugar in it has been used by the fermentation: it is also said to have 'fermented right out'.

Fermenting (or 'working'): The process brought about by yeast acting upon sugar to produce alcohol and carbon dioxide.

Fermentation trap (or air lock): A little gadget used to protect the fermentation from infection by the vinegar fly. Also called a 'bubbler'. A little water is placed in the trap of the airlock and as fermentation continues large bubbles of colourless carbon dioxide gas will be seen escaping.

Fining: Remove suspended solids from a cloudy wine by filtering or adding wine finings.

Flogger: A wooden tool for banging corks home.

Fortification: Increasing the strength of wine, beyond that possible by natural fermentation, by adding spirit.

Hydrometer: An instrument for measuring density of sugar in lb. and oz. per gallon, and the potential alcohol content of the must.

Lees: The deposit of yeast and solids formed during fermentation.

Liquor: The unfermented, sugar-containing liquid which will eventually be wine.

Must: The pulp or combination of basic ingredients from which a wine is made.

Nutrient: Nitrogenous matter (available in tablet form) added to the liquor to boost the action of the yeast; yeast food.

Pectic destroying enzymes: Many recipes recommend using one of these, e.g. Pektolase, Clearzyme, Pectinex. This is not essential; their use, however, not only assists in obtaining a clear wine, but also in extracting the greatest flavour from the fruit, etc.

Proof: Proof spirit contains 57·1% alcohol. 70° proof really means 70% of proof spirit. Thus ordinary proprietary bottles of spirit will contain only 40% alcohol by volume.

Racking: Siphoning the wine off the lees to clear and stabilize it.
Stable: A wine is said to be stable when there is no danger of
further fermentation.
Yeast: Most recipes suggest a particular variety of wine yeast that
will impart the best flavour and an appropriate alcohol content to
the wine to be made from these ingredients. But it does not follow
that this yeast only may be used. A general purpose wine yeast
may always be substituted if you prefer. The yeast should,
however, always be prepared in a starter bottle, see below, and
added to the must when it is thoroughly reactivated. The only
exception is when you use a ready prepared liquid yeast, which
you can put direct into the must.

Do not, at the outset, buy a lot of expensive equipment: it is
better to start making wine with what you have—you probably
have in your kitchen already some of the essentials—and then to
acquire the rest by stages. In time you will discover gadgets that
are especially useful, and you will also want to keep the articles you
take from your kitchen separate for the purpose of making wine.
Mashing vessels: First of all you need a container in which to
prepare your must. Earthenware crocks that have been glazed
inside are easy to clean, but heavy to move about, and it is best not
to use old or foreign crocks in case they have been lead glazed. A
plastic bucket or dustbin is the best buy on the market at present.
They are available in different sizes from a gallon upwards, usually
have lids that fit, have handles and are light to move, are easy to
clean, and do not affect the flavour of the wine. It is best to avoid
a metal container for any part of wine-making; as the acids in

the must could dissolve some of the metal and produce poison.

Masher: A long-handled wooden spoon would do at first, but a masher could be made with a block of wood that has a broom handle inserted into it. This could take the work out of breaking up berries and fruits.

A jug: One with a graduated measure for liquids is useful, and plastic is suggested again.

Strainer: You will need something in which to strain off the juice and press out the pulp. Muslin and nylon sieves can be used. But should you go in for large-scale wine-making you might get a handyman to make you a small press that can be used in conjunction with thoroughly cleaned flour bags.

Fermentation vessels: After straining and pressing you need containers in which to ferment your must. The one gallon jars with a narrow neck and 'ear' handles are the most popular. Remember to get rubber bungs and corks to fit.

Airlocks: It is worth getting as many of these as you can afford. They cost very little and are the wine-maker's best friend. Also called fermentation traps, they provide a barrier between the fermenting must and the outside air.

Siphon: For a shilling or two you can buy a length of rubber tubing about four feet long to use as a syphon, either for when you transfer liquid from one bottle to another, or for siphoning the wine off the yeast deposit.

Storage vessels: After racking, the fermented wine has to be stored for a time to mature. You can use the same jars as those in which fermentation has taken place, provided you keep them in the dark. Otherwise stoneware jars are very useful, or plastic containers in cardboard boxes. Wooden casks are ideal, but these need to be set on a stand and have wooden taps through which to siphon the wine away. You will need to collect empty wine bottles; and half gallon Winchesters are useful for storing purposes.

Corks: These should always be new, but you can buy plastic stoppers which are easily sterilized. Then, there is the Sandalands safety cork, in two sizes: for gallon jars, and standard wine bottles. A small safety valve on top allows gas to escape, and in the event of early bottling or further fermenting prevents bursting.

Funnels: These will be found useful at all times and it is worth while having several of varying sizes, although a plastic one about 6 inches across would be the best size for most purposes.

Bottle brush: A good bottle brush about 15 inches long costs very little and is an essential.

Refinements: As you progress in wine-making you will want to add other pieces of desirable equipment to your list, items such as: a thermometer, since it is often useful to know the termperature of your must. A hydrometer for calculating the strength of your wine. Glass tubing for taking samples. A corking device. Tie-on labels for jars and stick-on labels for bottles. Fancy labels are available for this last purpose and to give a professional finish you can also use plastic or metal foil bottle caps.

How to do it

Making wine can be summarized as follows:

1. Extract flavour from fruit or vegetables used.
2. Add sugar and yeast and ferment for up to 10 days in a bowl or crock, closely covered in a temperature of about 70°F.
3. Strain off, put into fermentation jars or bottles, filling to bottom of neck. Fit airlocks. Leave in temperature of about 60°F. This will be a quieter fermentation and will go on for some weeks.
4. Rack the cleared wine. Repeat this about two months later, and then a third time after another month or so. By then the wine should be stable, with no risk of burst bottles later on.
5. Bottle when the wine is about six months old. Store bottles on their sides, preferably in a room at 55°F., or below.

Preparation

The methods of preparation vary with the kind of wine being made. In most wines it is sufficient to wash the fruit, to break it up into small pieces and to pour boiling water on it. This mash is then left for a few days to soak so that the colour, flavour and goodness can be extracted. If any if the fruit is over-ripe, and in any case as a precaution against infection, it is a good rule always to add 1 Campden tablet per gallon. A pectic destroying enzyme will assist the process of extraction and help to produce a clear wine. While your fruit is soaking, or before, you will need to prepare your yeast.

Yeast in wine-making

You will often come across old recipes which do not give yeast as an ingredient. These depend upon the natural yeasts in the vegetable matter used, and should not, therefore, be relied upon; because the whole of wine-making practice really comes down to the matter of providing ideal conditions for the yeast, a living organism, to thrive and multiply. To do that the yeast must have sugar, it must have warmth, it must have oxygen, it must have a certain amount of nitrogenous matter, vitamins, and some acid. The ideal recipe will provide all these things; if any of them are lacking the ferment may 'stick', or temporarily stop.

Many wine-makers still use baker's or brewer's yeasts, but it is a pity to do so without having tried some of the excellent true wine yeasts now on the market. A good wine yeast has a high alcohol tolerance (i.e. it will allow the wine to ferment further and be that much stronger before it succumbs), it will form a firmer sediment, making racking simpler, and it will be less prone to impart 'off' flavours to the wine. It is possible to obtain Port, Sherry, Madeira, Burgundy, Tokay, Malaga, Sauterne, Pommard and Champagne yeasts, to mention a few. Naturally, it is advisable when using these specialised yeasts to employ them in 'musts' that will be sympathetic, i.e. Port or Burgundy yeast in a red wine such as elderberry, sloe, or damson, and a Champagne yeast in a sparkling wine. In the beginning, however, it might be best to experiment with a good general purpose wine yeast. One can also obtain a fairly good range of yeasts especially suitable for lager, beers and ale.

Preparing the yeast: If you do use a wine yeast, of whatever sort, it will usually have to be activated, and the principle is the same in most cases. Instead of adding the wine yeast direct to the must, it is started off in a half pint of fruit juice beforehand. The bottle to be used for this purpose must be carefully sterilized. The fruit juice—any fruit will do—is boiled with a tablespoon of sugar, the juice of a lemon and a small portion of nutrient. This is then poured into the prepared bottle which should never be more than half full, plugged with cotton wool and allowed to cool. When the temperature is down to 75°F. the yeast is added and the whole shaken up. The cotton-wool plug is replaced and the bottle is left in a warm place for a few days. Soon a splendid supply of bubbles will be seen rising to the surface and this means the yeast is alive and well. It may now be added to the must and fermentation will start almost immediately.

19

Maturation

When fermentation is completely finished the new wine will begin to clear from the top downwards and a thick deposit will be seen at the bottom of the jar. The first racking should now be made, by siphoning the wine into a clean jar and making sure that none of the residue accompanies it. The jar should be topped up with excess wine of the same ferment, with a similar type wine or with a little sugar dissolved in boiled water and allowed to cool. It is important that the jar should be well filled and that there is no large air space between the wine and well-fitting cork. You will find that most recipes for a gallon of wine make up to 10 pints, so that if you use a gallon jar for fermentation you will need a smaller jar for the residue. Keep it plugged with cotton wool as an airlock, and use it for topping up after racking. After two months the wine should be looked at again and a further deposit will be seen at the bottom of the jar. The wine will look much clearer now. Rack it again and top up as before. Repeat this process in a month or two. Then the final racking can be made when the wine is bottled—about six months after the end of fermentation.

Grape wines

Although it is widely accepted today that wine can be made from innumerable fruits, flowers, vegetables and grains, etc., the original meaning of the word wine is 'the fermented juice of fresh grapes', and undoubtedly grapes are the easiest fruit from which to make wine. White wine can be made from white and black grapes, the method being to express the juice and ferment it alone. Red wine, on the other hand, is produced by leaving the skins of the crushed black grapes in the must, so that the colour from them is extracted. If the skins are left in only one or two days a *vin rosé* will be produced; if longer, a wine of a much deeper colour; but it is unwise to leave them more than 10 days before drawing off the liquid.

Grape juice concentrate can be bought for both red and white wine. The quality varies and it is advisable to buy the best, but excellent results can be obtained by following directions given. The method of fermentation is the same as with other wines, and a yeast culture is usually supplied with the concentrate. These wines can greatly improve other wines and are strongly recommended for blending.

White wine

18 lb. of seedless grapes, cheap and plentiful in July and August, will make 2 gallons of excellent wine.

Pick the grapes over carefully, removing any that are bad and taking out the stalks. Rinse the loose grapes to remove dirt and dust and crush them well in your hands, making sure to break each fruit. Pour off the juice, put the pulp into a clean cloth and squeeze out remaining juice. Put the pulp into a mashing vessel and pour on 6 pints of boiling water, stir, cover and leave for two days. You should have extracted about 10 pints of juice from the grapes. Put this into a fermentation jar with 2 Campden tablets and fit an airlock. A yeast starter should be prepared with the yeast of your choice, but in the first instance a general purpose wine yeast might be advisable. Later, you can experiment with Burgundy, Sauternes, Sherry yeasts, etc., but they will require different amounts of sugar and vary in their maturing times, but your results should resemble the wines to which the selected yeast is indigenous. After two days' soaking, strain and press the grapes strenuously and add the strained liquid to the grape juice. Sugar is now added, and for a good all-purpose wine $1\frac{1}{2}$ lb. to the gallon should be sufficient, but later, when you have a hydrometer, you can first of all test the amount of sugar in the must and add according to the type of wine you plan. The yeast should also be added, and the fermentation trap fitted. Put the jar in a warm place. After fermenting, rack three times over a period of six months, and store and use after it is one year old.

Red wine

Use black grapes, prepare as above, but after crushing each berry leave the skins in the juice from 2–8 days according to the colour required. A couple of crushed Campden tablets per gallon of juice should be stirred in and the vessel very well covered. Stir the must twice a day since the skins float on the surface and tend to dry out. After straining and pressing, the pulp can again be soaked in some boiling water. When liquid is strained from the pulp and added to the juice, add 1 lb. sugar per gallon of liquid and the yeast, fit airlocks. When fermenting starts to slow add another ½ lb. per gallon dissolved in some of the wine. To preserve its colour it is best to have an opaque or coloured fermenting jar. Similarly, when bottling for storing, use coloured bottles. Rack as above and use after a year.

Flower wines

All flower wines are made in much the same way, so that the following recipe will make a gallon of wine and flowers added will give it its bouquet and flavour. On the whole, because flower wines are so sweet smelling, they are better if slightly sweet.

You will need:

FLOWERS	8 OZ. CHOPPED RAISINS
1 GALLON OF WATER	3 LB. SUGAR
RIND AND JUICE OF 1 LEMON	GENERAL PURPOSE WINE YEAST
1 ORANGE, 1 GRAPEFRUIT	NUTRIENT TABLET

Gather the flowers on a warm sunny day, when the petals are open. Remove petals from the green sepals, because the sepals can give an unpleasant flavour to the wine. Pour boiling water on the flowers and add the fruit rinds. Steep this mash for 4 days in a closely covered vessel, pressing down and crushing it twice daily. Strain and press out all the liquid. Stir in chopped raisins, sugar, fruit juice, yeast and nutrient. Ferment in the usual way, removing the raisins by straining and pressing after 7 days. Continue fermentation, rack and mature and serve as a sweet wine.

Amounts of flower required:

Elderflower: 1 pint of well pressed-down florets, freshly picked.
Carnations: 2 quarts white 'pinks' petals.
Clover: 2 quarts purple clover.
Dandelion: 2 quarts dandelion heads.
Cowslips: 2 quarts cowslip flowers.
Marigold: 2 quarts marigold heads.
Rose petal: 2 quarts dark red sweet-smelling rose petals.
Primroses: 2 quarts fresh primroses.
Hawthorn blossom: 2 quarts fresh hawthorn flowers, pink or white.
Golden rod: 2 handfuls of blossom.

Fruit, vegetable and other wines

Here are recipes for wines covering a wide field. There are many more, but when you have made some of these you will, doubtless, see endless possibilities with other ingredients, and be ready to experiment. All wines require fermenting, racking and maturing as previously described in this chapter.

Apple wine

12–14 LB. WINDFALL APPLES
1 GALLON WATER
1 CAMPDEN TABLET
1 TEASPOON PEKTOLASE

$1\frac{1}{2}$–$2\frac{1}{2}$ LB. SUGAR
YEAST IN VARIETY OF CHOICE:
   GRAVES, SAUTERNES, ETC.
NUTRIENT

Wash apples and remove any bad portions. Mince or better still crush the apples and add them to a gallon of cold water in which the Campden tablet has been dissolved. Sprinkle in the Pektolase. Soak for 3 to 4 days. Strain and squeeze the pulp dry. Add sugar to the liquid. The quantity will vary according to the sweetness of the apples and the type of wine you want to achieve; a hydrometer would be useful here. Add the prepared yeast and nutrient. Apple must takes to yeast well, and it is well worth experimenting with different varieties.

Celery wine

4 LB. CELERY STALKS WITHOUT LEAVES

1 GALLON WATER

$2\frac{3}{4}$ LB. SUGAR

GERMAN YEAST

NUTRIENT

Chop up the washed celery and boil in water until tender. Strain well, stir sugar into the liquor and when cool add the activated yeast and nutrient. This can be served as a medium sweet wine.

Carrot wine

4 LB. GOOD CARROTS

1 GALLON WATER

RIND AND JUICE OF 1 LARGE LEMON

RIND AND JUICE OF 1 ORANGE

RIND AND JUICE OF 1 GRAPE-FRUIT

1 CAMPDEN TABLET

1 TEASPOON PEKTOLASE

$3\frac{1}{2}$ LB. SUGAR

8 OZ. RAISINS

SHERRY OR GENERAL PURPOSE YEAST

NUTRIENT

Scrub and grate the carrots. Boil them for 10 minutes with the lemon, orange and grapefruit rinds. Strain and when cool add the Campden tablet and the Pektolase to the liquor. Cover and leave for 24 hours. Stir in the sugar, chopped raisins, fruit juice, fermenting yeast and nutrient. Remove raisins from fermenting liquor after 7 days, allow fermentation to continue.

Canary banana wine

4 LB. PEELED BANANAS, A FEW BANANA SKINS IN GOOD CONDITION

1 GALLON WATER

3 LB. SUGAR

4 OZ. RAISINS

RIND AND JUICE OF 1 LARGE 　　GENERAL PURPOSE WINE YEAST
　LEMON 　　　　　　　　　　　NUTRIENT
RIND AND JUICE OF 1 SEVILLE
　ORANGE

Put the peeled bananas, banana skins, lemon and orange rinds into
a cotton bag and boil in water for half an hour. Strain and press
well. Stir the sugar into the liquor and the chopped raisins, and
when cool add the orange and lemon juice, the fermenting yeast
and nutrient. Strain raisins from the fermenting jar after about 10
days, leaving the liquor to continue fermenting.

Cherry wine

6 LB. CHERRIES (RED AND 　　1 CAMPDEN TABLET
　WHITE) 　　　　　　　　　　2$\frac{1}{2}$ LB. SUGAR
1 GALLON WATER 　　　　　　BORDEAUX YEAST
1 TEASPOON PEKTOLASE 　　　NUTRIENT

Stalk and wash cherries, pour boiling water on to them and when
cool mash fruit throughly. Add Pektolase and Campden tablet,
cover and leave to soak for 2 days. Strain and press. Stir sugar
into the liquor and add fermenting yeast and nutrient. Serve as
a dry table wine.

Damson wine

4 LB. SOUND RIPE DAMSONS 　　3$\frac{1}{2}$ LB. SUGAR
1 GALLON BOILING WATER 　　　PORT YEAST
1 TEASPOON PEKTOLASE 　　　　NUTRIENT
1 CAMPDEN TABLET

Stalk and wash fruit. Pour on the boiling water and when cool
mash the fruit well. Add Pektolase and Campden tablet. Cover
and leave to soak for 3 days. Strain and press. Stir 3 lb. of sugar into
liquor and add the yeast and nutrient. Add the rest of the sugar,
dissolved in a little of the liquor during fermentation. Mature for
18 months and serve as sweet wine.

Date wine

4 LB. DATES	RIND AND JUICE OF 1 GRAPE-
1 GALLON WATER	FRUIT
RIND AND JUICE OF 2 LARGE	2 LB. SUGAR
LEMONS	SHERRY YEAST
RIND AND JUICE OF 1 SEVILLE	NUTRIENT
ORANGE	

Chop the dates and boil them gently with the fruit rinds and 6 date stones for $\frac{1}{2}$ hour. Strain off liquor. Stir in sugar and when cool add the fruit juice, yeast and nutrient. Ferment for as long as possible, add extra sugar if necessary. Keep for 2 years before serving. Strong and sweet like a cream sherry.

Elderberry wine

3 LB. FRESH ELDERBERRIES	JUICE OF 1 LARGE LEMON
1 GALLON WATER	BURGUNDY YEAST
2$\frac{1}{2}$ LB. SUGAR	NUTRIENT

Stalk and wash the berries. Mash them thoroughly. Pour boiling water over them and leave to soak for 4 days. Strain and press out liquor. Add sugar, lemon juice, yeast and nutrient and ferment to dryness.

Gooseberry wine

5 LB. HARD GREEN	1 TEASPOON PEKTOLASE
GOOSEBERRIES	2$\frac{1}{2}$ LB. SUGAR
1 GALLON BOILING WATER	GERMAN YEAST
1 CAMPDEN TABLET	NUTRIENT

Top and tail and wash gooseberries. Pour boiling water over them and when cool, crush the berries with your hands without breaking pips. Add Campden tablet and Pektolase, cover and soak for 2 days. Strain and press, stir in sugar, fermenting yeast and nutrient. Left to mature for a year this wine closely resembles a Hock. To make a sparkling wine: Same ingredients and method as above except that you use 3 lb. sugar and a Champagne yeast. When the wine is clear bottle it in strong bottles, add a teaspoon of sugar to each and wire down the corks.

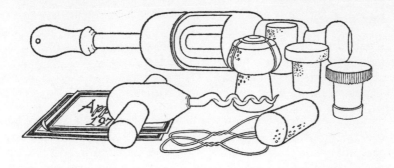

Ginger wine

2 OZ. ROOT GINGER	3 LB. SUGAR
1 GALLON BOILING WATER	1 LB. RAISINS
½ TEASPOON CAYENNE PEPPER	GENERAL PURPOSE YEAST
RIND AND JUICE OF 2 LEMONS	NUTRIENT
RIND AND JUICE OF 2 ORANGES	

Crush the ginger and boil with the pepper and fruit rinds for 20 minutes. Strain on to the sugar and chopped raisins and stir well. When cool add the fruit juice, yeast and nutrient. After one week strain and press the raisins and continue fermentation. Serve as a sweet wine.

Marrow wine

5 LB. RIPE MARROW	1 OZ. GINGER
RIND AND JUICE OF 1 LARGE LEMON	4 OZ. RAISINS
	1 GALLON BOILING WATER
RIND AND JUICE OF 1 LARGE ORANGE	3 LB. SUGAR
	GENERAL PURPOSE YEAST
RIND AND JUICE OF 1 GRAPE-FRUIT	NUTRIENT

Wipe marrow clean, and grate it coarsely (incuding seeds) into a mashing vessel. Add fruit rinds, bruised ginger and chopped raisins. Pour on boiling water, stir and cover. When cool add sugar, fruit juice, yeast and nutrient. Ferment on the pulp for 4 days, pressing it down twice daily. Strain and press and continue fermentation.

Parsnip wine

4 LB. PARSNIPS	3 LB. SUGAR
RIND AND JUICE OF 2 LEMONS	8 OZ. RAISINS
RIND AND JUICE OF 2 ORANGES	SHERRY YEAST
I GALLON OF WATER	NUTRIENT

Parsnips dug in January are the best for wine. Scrub, remove bad and rusty portions, dice. Boil together with the fruit rinds until parsnips are just tender. Strain, stir sugar into liquor, add chopped raisins, fruit juice, yeast and nutrient. Continue fermenting with a little added sugar for as long as possible. Keep to mature for 18 months and rack several times during this period.

Your own cider

It is almost impossible to make apple cider without a press or similar device. A mixture of varieties of ripe cider apples should be used and allowed to mellow until they are soft. Wash the fruit and put it in a tub or polythene dustbin and crush it with a

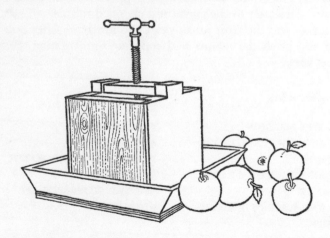

masher (a heavy length of timber). Then express the juice by means of a press or by wrapping the fruit a little at a time in a stout cloth and running it through a mangle. Collect the juice in fermenting jars. Add 2 Campden tablets per gallon of juice. If you want a sweet cider add sugar, about 8 oz. per gallon. Add a general purpose or champagne yeast with nutrient tablet and allow to ferment to dryness. Rack in beer bottles and prime with a scant teaspoon of sugar per pint bottle. Mature for at least 3 months, but do not keep for longer than 9 months.

You will require 15 to 20 lb. of apples to make a gallon of cider. *Note:* Perry is a similar drink made with pears.

Home-brewed beer

Although not as ancient a drink as mead, ale was made and drunk in this country long before the Romans came. At that time it was a fermented liquor made from a cereal mash of barley, wheat or rye. The Romans, whom we have so much to be grateful for, also introduced the hop, although our forebears were slow to welcome it. As a result ale was still the drink for many centuries and when hops were added it was called beer.

Hops were introduced to stabilize and flavour the beer; the resin in the hops acts as a preservative, which helps prevent the beer from going sour. It also adds the bitterness to beer. There are now several varieties of hops with very different types of bitterness and flavour, the brewer selects these carefully depending upon the type of beer he wishes to produce.

The basic ingredients in beer are hops for bitterness, malt and sugar to give the strength, and yeast which breaks down the malt sugars into alcohol and carbon dioxide gas. A simple water treatment: adding Brewer's Gypsum to the water helps to reduce the malty tang often associated with home-brewed beers.

For years the type of hops available to the home brewer were almost always the ones the brewer rejected, but specialist suppliers can now obtain the best grades for you. These have names: a Kent Golding is good for bitters and pale ale; a Fuggle Hop for milds and stouts, and Bavarian Hallertaur for lager. There are many others and breweries often use a combination of two or three different types.

When making beer ensure that anything which comes into contact with it has been carefully washed and sterilized. Bacteria can easily breed and turn the brew sour. A strong solution of Milton can be used, but there are several special brewing sterilizers on the market.

Basic equipment: a large pan, a plastic dustbin to hold 5 gallons, 4 feet of food grade $\frac{5}{16}$ inch bore plastic tubing, beer bottles or screw-topped lemonade bottles (avoid using squash bottles, they can explode), a muslin boiling bag. Do not use metal containers unless made of stainless steel.

To make 5 gallons:

Bitter	Mild	Lager
3 OZ. GOLDING HOPS	2 OZ. FUGGLES	2 OZ HALLERTAUR
1 LB. CRYSTALGRAIN MALT	8 OZ. CRYSTAL MALT GRAIN	1 LB. LAGER GRAIN MALT
2 TEASPOONS BREWER'S GYPSUM	2 OZ. ROASTED BARLEY GRAIN	2 TEASPOONS BREWER'S GYPSUM
3 LB. GRANULATED SUGAR	2 TEASPOONS BREWER'S GYPSUM	3 LB. GRANULATED SUGAR
2 LB. SFX MALT EXTRACT	3 LB. GRANULATED SUGAR	2 LB. DMS MALT EXTRACT
1 TOP FERMENTING YEAST	2 LB. SFX MALT EXTRACT	1 BOTTOM FERMENTING YEAST
	1 TOP FERMENTING YEAST	

Place hops and grain malts in muslin boiling bag and tie end. Add gypsum to 8 pints of boiling water, and place boiling bag with contents into pan with water and boil vigorously for 45 minutes. Add sugar and malt extract. Remove boiling bag, and pour boiling liquid into your bin and add cold water to make up to 5 gallons. Stir and allow to cool to 70°F. Add yeast when liquid is cool. Never add yeast before liquid has cooled or the heat will damage it and prevent fermentation. Keep in a room or cupboard at 65°–70°F. Fermentation will be completed in 6 days. This time may be longer in cold weather or a day or so shorter in hot weather. With bitter and mild ale skim yeast froth after 24 hours. Take care that fermentation is completed before bottling as failure to do this could result in burst bottles. When the surface of the brew is quite still and only the odd yeast floater can be observed, use a sterilized spoon and taste it. If the brew does not taste sweet fermentation is completed, but if sweet allow another day and test again.

Syphon the beer into the bottles to within an inch of the top. Do not overfill as this can cause burst bottles. Add 1 level teaspoon sugar per pint, this produces secondary fermentation and gives the beer added sparkle. Before screwing on bottle tops, check that rubber rings are in good condition, replace if damaged or worn; check bottles for cracks.

When you serve your beer pour out of the bottle in one steady stage. Stop pouring when sediment is seen to rise, and with a little practice a crystal clear glass can be poured every time. The beer may be sampled after a week, but it improves with keeping and will not be at its best until 3 weeks after bottling.

There are many simpler recipes for beer, but by taking the trouble to obtain the more sophisticated ingredients, you will ensure stable results.

Ginger beer

2 LEMONS	I GALLON BOILING WATER
I OZ. BRUISED ROOT GINGER	I LEVEL TEASPOON GRANULATED
I LB. SUGAR	YEAST
¼ OZ. CREAM OF TARTAR	

Carefully peel off the zest of the 2 lemons and break up and crush the ginger. Add the sugar and cream of tartar and pour on the boiling water. Stir well. Remove and discard the white pith of the lemons, then cut lemons into thin wafers and float these on the water. Cover with a cloth and when cool sprinkle on the yeast. Re-cover and leave for 2 days. Strain off the yeast, strain out the ginger and lemon, bottle in screw-top bottles, leave for 3 days.

Nettle beer

2 GALLONS YOUNG NETTLES	2 OZ. HOPS
I OZ. ROOT GINGER	4 OZ. SARSAPARILLA
2 GALLONS WATER	1½ LB. CASTER SUGAR
4 LB. MALT	I OZ. CREAMED YEAST

Wash nettles well and bruise ginger. Put into a pan with water, malt, hops and sarsaparilla. Boil for 15 minutes and strain over sugar. Stir until sugar dissolves, then add yeast. Leave to ferment. Make sure fermentation is finished before pouring into bottles, cork and tie down with string. This beer is suitable for drinking in about a week.

Mead

Cave paintings of 12,000 years ago show men collecting honey from a hive of bees. It was the original sweetener, and how long it took Man to discover it could become a fermented drink we do not know. However, although thousands of years of history went into the making of mead, wine made from fermented grapes eventually supplanted it.

There are many different kinds of honey, light and dark, thin and thick, and the flavour depends a lot upon the kinds of flowers visited by the bees. In spite of the subtle differences in flavour the chemical composition of honeys remains fairly constant.

Three or four pounds of honey will be required to make a gallon of mead, depending upon whether you want a dry mead, not too strongly flavoured, or one that is sweeter and stronger. The light honey is preferable to the dark, which can give too pronounced a flavour. In the process of preparation you bring the honey slowly to the boil in at least an equal amount of water and simmer it gently for 15 minutes or so until the impurities rise to the surface as a scum which can be skimmed and thrown away.

Half an ounce each of citric and tartaric acid is needed and twice as much nutrient as necessary for wine.

Strictly speaking, any other ingredients apart from yeast make mead something rather than mead: e.g. mead containing spices is called Methaglyn—a Celtic word. And yet a little ginger added can sharpen the flavour without altering it. A variety of yeasts can be used, but a special honey yeast—Maury—gives a better flavour.

Fermentation is carried on in the same way as wine, though it usually lasts much longer, six months or so. It is important to keep the fermenting liquor in a warm and even temperature the whole time. When fermentation is finished mead needs to be racked and stored for as long as possible—2 years or more.

Dry mead: 3½ lb. white honey, juice and rind 2 large lemons, 6 pints water, 1 cup cold tea, 2 tablets yeast nutrient, Maury yeast.
Sweet mead or Sac: 4½ lb. white honey, juice and rind of 3 large lemons, 8 oz. white sugar, 5 pints water, 1 cup cold tea, 2 tablets yeast nutrient, Maury yeast or Sherry yeast.
Methaglyn: 4½ lb. white honey, juice and rind of 3 large lemons, 8 oz. demerara sugar, 5 pints water, 1 cup cold tea, ½ oz. root ginger, 6 cloves, good grating of nutmeg or cinnamon, 2 tablets yeast nutrient, Maury yeast. (Serve slightly warm.)

32

2

Jams, jellies and marmalades

Jam-making is one of those old country arts which, like bottling, enables the country housewife to put summer in store, and enjoy delicious fruits all through the winter. During Victorian times the word 'jam' was thought to be rather vulgar, and ladies preferred to describe it as a preserve or conserve. Old family recipes, carefully inscribed in fat exercise books, and handed down from one generation of farmers' wives to the next, are often so described.

Almost every housewife has her favourite recipes for the jams she makes every year. Sometimes the result is more successful, or less so, than it has been in previous years, for various reasons. Oddly enough, if we have had a good summer, and the fruit is riper than usual, the jam will not set so well and has less of the distinctive rich fruit flavour.

The recipes given here are well tried and tested, and they will generally give an excellent result. They include many for less usual fruits, one for green tomato and apple, and one for a delicious and delicate conserve made with rose petals.

Many a farmer's wife has told me that the old-fashioned red cabbage rose has the sweetest perfume, makes the best rose petal jam, the finest crystallized flowers for cake decoration, the most richly scented pot-pourri, and perhaps even more important, the most potent sweet *rosé* wine.

B

Pectin content of fruit

Before making a jam or jelly it is important to know whether the fruit to be used has a high or low pectin content. Pectin is a natural gum-like substance, found in varying degrees in all fruit, which is essential to the setting of jams, jellies and marmalades. Below are a few examples of fruits which are relatively high, medium and low in pectin.

Fruits high in pectin include apples, blackcurrants, gooseberries, oranges, lemons, plums and redcurrants. Fruits with a medium pectin content include apricots, blackberries, raspberries and loganberries. Fruits with a low pectin content include cherries and strawberries. If you are unsure of the pectin content of a fruit it is possible to carry out a simple test. Put a teaspoon of juice from the cooked fruit together with 3 teaspoons of methylated spirit. If the fruit is high in pectin a firm jelly-like lump will form; if the fruit has only a moderate amount two or three soft lumps will form; and if the fruit is very low in pectin it will form a lot of very small pieces.

There are several ways of overcoming the problem of making jams from fruits with a low pectin content. Firstly the fruit can be mixed with another that is high in pectin. For example, apple and blackberry, raspberry and redcurrant. Secondly, juice of high pectin fruit can be added; and thirdly a commercial pectin, such as Certo, can be used.

Fruit for jam should be firm and ripe, but it is important that it should not be over-ripe, as the jam does not set and the flavour tends to be indistinct and too sweet.

The choice of pan is very important in jam- and jelly-making. If a lot of jam is made it is worth while investing in a special pan for the purpose. Always use a pan which is sufficiently large. It should not be more than half full when the sugar is added to the fruit, because the mixture must boil rapidly without risk of boiling over. A pressure pan must never be more than half filled when ready for pressure-cooking jams.

The old copper preserving pan makes wonderful jam, but do remember to wash it thoroughly to remove any hint of metal polish which may have crept into the interior. A wide, fairly shallow pan of aluminium, stainless steel or enamel is ideal, preferably with a heavy base. Jam tends to stick and burn in a pan

34

with a thin base. Iron or zinc pans should not be used. The acid in the fruit when it comes in contact with the metal will cause loss of colour and flavour.

To prevent jam from sticking, and forming unnecessary scum, rub the preserving pan inside the base with butter, or a little glycerine, before adding the fruit. If much scum forms, stir a small knob of butter into it. Use a long-handled wooden spoon, as fast-boiling jam often throws out drops which cause painful burns to the hands.

Method of making jam

The method for making jam is basically the same for all recipes· First the fruit is prepared and put into the pan, with water if needed, and simmered gently until the fruit is soft. Sometimes no water is added, but a little lemon juice to help the set. The sugar (either preserving, granulated or loaf) is added to the pan and the mixture is stirred over a low heat until the sugar has dissolved. It is most important that the jam does not boil before the sugar dissolves as this causes the sugar to crystallize. The jam is then allowed to boil rapidly without stirring until setting point is reached. This can take anything from 5 to 20 minutes according to the fruit and type of pan used. An indication that setting point has been reached is that high frothing ceases and the boiling becomes noisy with heavy plopping bubbles.

There are several ways of testing for a set, the four most commonly used being given here. When using the first or second methods, remove the jam from the heat while the test is carried out or it may go beyond the desired stage, in which case it may never set or may form a sticky toffee-like mixture.

Tests for setting point

1. Cold Plate test: Spoon a little jam on to a cold plate, allow to cool. If setting point has been reached, the surface will set and wrinkle when pushed with the fingertip.

2. Flake test: Dip a clean wooden spoon into the jam, remove it and twirl gently to cool the jam. Then tilt the spoon to allow surplus jam to run off. If the jam has reached setting point, it will set on the spoon and the drops will run together to form flakes.

3. Temperature test: Use a sugar thermometer, dipping it into hot water immediately before and after use. Stir the jam, insert the thermomenter and fix securely. A good set should be obtained when the temperature reaches 220°F.

4. Volume test: This works on the basis that 3 lb. sugar will make 5 lb. jam. Therefore if you use 3 lb. sugar and expect a 5 lb. yield, pour the contents of 5 1 lb. jars into your pan and mark the level of the water on the handle of a wooden spoon. Empty out the water and make the jam in the usual way. In this case setting point should be reached when the level of the contents of the pan corresponds to the mark on the handle of the spoon.

Jam must be removed from the heat immediately when setting point is reached. Over-boiling darkens the colour as well as affecting the consistency of the jam. If making a jelly or purée type jam it should be poured into hot sterilized jars immediately. If making a whole fruit jam or marmalade allow to cool for 5 to 20 minutes, and stir before potting. This ensures that the fruit remains evenly distributed in the jar. Fill to within $\frac{1}{4}$ inch of the top, cover with a waxed paper circle. Wipe any jam off the sides of the jars while it is still warm. When cold the jars can be covered with cellophane or pliofilm, labelled with the type of jam and the date made, and stored in a cool dry place.

Here are some recipes for simple jams which are frequently made in small quantities, and are particularly successful because the fruit used has excellent setting qualities.

Fig and lemon jam

2 LB. DRIED FIGS

1$\frac{1}{2}$ PINTS HOT WATER

JUICE OF 2 LEMONS

3 LB. GRANULATED SUGAR

Wash the figs and soak in cold water overnight. Rinse in fresh water and cut into small pieces, removing any hard bits of stem. Put into a preserving pan with hot water and simmer until tender. Stir in the lemon juice and sugar and put over a low heat until the sugar has dissolved. Boil rapidly until setting point is reached, then pour into hot sterilized jars. Cover tightly. **Yields about 6 lb.**

Huckleberry jam

I LB. HUCKLEBERRIES   2 LB. GRANULATED SUGAR
4 TABLESPOONS WATER   JUICE OF 2 LEMONS

Wash the huckleberries and put into a preserving pan with the water. Simmer gently until soft. Stir in the sugar and lemon juice and keep over a low heat until the sugar has dissolved, then boil rapidly until setting point is reached. Pour into hot sterilized jars and cover. **Yields about 2½ lb.**

Japonica jam

I LB. JAPONICAS   SUGAR
I PINT WATER   LEMONS
PINCH GROUND GINGER

Wash japonicas, but do not peel or core. Put into a preserving pan or large saucepan with the water (if the fruit is under-ripe add an extra ¼ pint water) and ginger. Simmer gently until the mixture is a pulp. Sieve the pulp and to each I lb. of pulp add I lb. sugar and the juice of 2 lemons. Put over a low heat until sugar has dissolved, then boil rapidly until setting point is reached. Pour into hot sterilized jars and cover. **Yields about 2 lb.**

Plum jam

3 LB. PLUMS   ¼–¾ PINT WATER
3 LB. SUGAR

Remove the stalks and put the washed plums into a pan with the water. Sweet, juicy plums will need only ¼ pint water, but the hard cooking variety will need about ¾ pint. Simmer gently until the fruit is well broken down. Stir in the sugar and cook over a low heat, then boil rapidly. Remove the plum stones as they rise to the surface. When setting point is reached, remove from the heat, skim and pour into hot sterilized jars. Cover tightly. If liked a few blanched plum kernels can be added with the sugar. **Yields about 5 lb.**

Note: If stone fruit such as plums are slightly under-ripe, it is difficult to remove the stones. Leave some or all of the stones in the fruit, and as the jam boils they will rise to the surface and can be skimmed off with a perforated spoon. A metal sieve hooked over the side of the preserving pan above the surface of the boiling jam is most useful, as the stones can be scooped into it and allowed to drip surplus jam back into the pan.

Green tomato and apple jam

I LB. GREEN TOMATOES	2 TABLESPOONS VINEGAR
I LB. COOKING APPLES	2 TABLESPOONS WATER
1¼ LB. GRANULATED SUGAR	

Thinly slice the tomatoes; peel, core and chop the apples. Put all the ingredients into a preserving pan, mix well and leave for 1–2 days until it becomes a syrupy mass. Put over a low heat until the sugar is dissolved, then boil rapidly until setting point is reached. Pour into hot sterilized jars and cover tightly. Keep for a few weeks before eating. **Yields about 2½ lb.**

Rose petal jam

I LB. ROSE PETALS	8 OZ. HONEY
8 OZ. SUGAR	4 TABLESPOONS WATER

Put the well washed rose petals and the remaining ingredients into a preserving pan and cook over a gentle heat until the sugar has dissolved. Bring to the boil and boil until setting point is reached. Pour into hot sterilized jars and cover tightly. **Yields about 1½ lb.**

Note: The petals may be gathered over two or three days. They should be put into a deep crock with a little lemon juice sprinkled over them and the crock should be kept covered.

Raspberry jam

6 LB. RASPBERRIES	6 LB. GRANULATED SUGAR

Hull raspberries (remove stems), put into a preserving pan, heat slowly. Do not add any water, but squash some of the fruit near the base of the pan to help break it up. Bring to the boil and simmer gently for about 5 minutes. Add the sugar and heat gently until it has dissolved, then boil rapidly until setting point is reached— about 5 minutes. Pour into hot sterilized jars and cover tightly. **Yields about 10 lb.**

Morello cherry jam

3 LB. MORELLO CHERRIES	3 LB. SUGAR
¼ PINT WATER	1 BOTTLE COMMERCIAL PECTIN
3 TABLESPOONS LEMON JUICE	

Wash and stone the cherries and put into a preserving pan with the water and lemon juice. Simmer with the lid on for 15 minutes or until the fruit is tender. Add the sugar and cook over a low heat until dissolved, then bring to a rolling boil and boil rapidly for 3 minutes. Remove from heat, stir, add pectin and leave for about 15 minutes before bottling so that the fruit is evenly distributed. Pour into hot sterilized jars and cover tightly. **Yields about 5 lb.**
Note : Although there is a special gadget on the market for stoning cherries, here is the old farmhouse method. Use a strong new

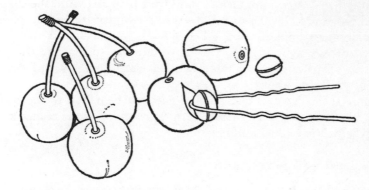

hairpin. Insert the rounded end into the cherry. Move gently around until you feel it lock around the stone, then pull sharply towards you. This will bring the stone out with the hairpin. Hold the cherry over the preserving pan or a basin, as the juice tends to spurt out with the stone.

Strawberry jam

2¼ LB. STRAWBERRIES
3 TABLESPOONS LEMON JUICE
3 LB. GRANULATED SUGAR

KNOB BUTTER
½ BOTTLE COMMERCIAL PECTIN

Hull the strawberries, wash and cut in half if large or leave whole if small. Put into a preserving pan with the lemon juice and sugar and leave for 1 hour, stirring occasionally. Place over a low heat and stir continuously. When the sugar has dissolved, add the butter which reduces foaming. Bring to the boil and boil rapidly for 4 minutes, stirring occasionally. Remove from heat, add the pectin and stir well. Allow to cool for at least 20 minutes before bottling to prevent fruit rising to the top. Pour into hot sterilized jars and cover. **Yields about 5 lb.**

Apricot jam

2 LB. RIPE APRICOTS
¼ PINT WATER
3 TABLESPOONS LEMON JUICE

3 LB. SUGAR
½ BOTTLE COMMERCIAL PECTIN

Wash, halve and stone the fruit, but do not peel. Put into a preserving pan with water and lemon juice, cover and simmer gently for about 20 minutes or until fruit is tender. Add the sugar and cook over a low heat until dissolved. Bring to the boil and boil rapidly for 1 minute, stirring occasionally. Remove from the heat and stir in pectin. Cool for about 10 minutes so that the fruit is evenly distributed, then pour into hot sterilized jars and cover tightly. **Yields about 5 lb.**

Note : If liked, a few blanched kernels can be added to the fruit when it is cooking. To blanch kernels, crack open the stones and dip kernels in boiling water.

Rhubarb and ginger jam

4 LB. RHUBARB
4 LB. GRANULATED SUGAR

8 OZ. CRYSTALLIZED GINGER, CHOPPED
GRATED ZEST AND JUICE OF 4 LARGE LEMONS

Wash the rhubarb and cut into 1-inch pieces. Put into a casserole with 1 lb. sugar and cook in a slow oven, for about 20 minutes, or until the fruit is soft but not broken. Put the rhubarb into a preserving pan with the remaining ingredients and cook over a low heat until the sugar has dissolved. Boil rapidly until setting point is reached, about 30 minutes. Pour into hot sterilized jars and cover tightly. **Yields 5–6 lb.**

Variation : Rhubarb and mixed peel jam can be made by replacing ginger with 8 oz. chopped mixed candied peel.

Hedgerow jam

8 OZ. ROSE HIPS	1 LB. BLACKBERRIES
8 OZ. HAWS	1 LB. ELDERBERRIES
8 OZ. ROWANBERRIES	4 OZ. HAZELNUTS
8 OZ. SLOES	SUGAR
1 LB. CRAB APPLES	

Wash and clean the fruit well. Put the rose hips, haws, rowan-berries, sloes and chopped crab apples in a preserving pan, add water to cover, cook until all are tender. Sieve and weigh the pulp. Put the pulp into a pan with the blackberries, elderberries and chopped nuts and simmer for about 15 minutes. Add 2 lb. sugar plus the weight of the hip pulp. Cook over a low heat until the sugar has dissolved, then boil rapidly until setting point is reached. Pour into hot sterilized jars and cover. **Yields 5–6 lb.**

Apple ginger jam

3 LB. APPLES	JUICE OF 1 LEMON
1 OZ. ROOT GINGER	3 LB. GRANULATED SUGAR
1 PINT WATER	4 OZ. CRYSTALLIZED GINGER

Wash the apples, peel, core and cut up. Bruise the root ginger, tie in a piece of muslin with apple peel and cores. Put the apples, water, lemon juice and muslin bag into a preserving pan and cook until apples are tender. Remove muslin bag, squeezing gently to extract pectin. Add sugar and chopped crystallized ginger. Put over a low heat until sugar has dissolved, then boil rapidly until setting point is reached. Pour into hot sterilized jars and cover tightly. **Yields about 5 lb.**

Melon and lemon jam

5½ LB. MELON   3 LB. SUGAR
4 LEMONS

Peel the melon and remove the pips, reserving these. Chop the melon flesh. Peel zest of lemons and squeeze juice. Tie lemon zest and pips and melon pips in a muslin bag and put into a preserving pan with the melon. Cook very gently until the melon is tender, about 40 minutes. Remove the muslin bag, squeezing gently to extract the pectin, and add the lemon juice and sugar. Cook over a low heat until sugar is dissolved, then boil rapidly until setting point is reached. Pour into hot sterilized jars and cover tightly. **Yields about 5 lb.**

Rose hip and apple jam

1 LB. ROSE HIPS   1 LB. APPLES
1½ PINTS WATER   1 LB. SUGAR

Wash the hips well and put into a preserving pan with water. Simmer for 2 hours. Put into a jelly bag and leave to strain overnight. Peel, core and slice the apples, add to juice and cook until pulped. Stir in the sugar and cook over a low heat until dissolved. Bring to the boil and boil rapidly until setting point is reached. Pour into hot sterilized jars and cover tightly. **Yields about 2 lb.**

Chestnut jam

2 LB. CHESTNUTS   3 TEASPOONS VANILLA ESSENCE
1 LB. SUGAR   ½ PINT WATER

Make a slit in each chestnut and boil for about 20 minutes or until they can be easily peeled. Peel and sieve. Put the sugar, vanilla and water into a pan and place over a low heat until sugar has dissolved. Add the chestnuts and cook until stiff. Put into hot sterilized jars and cover tightly. **Yields about 2½ lb.**

Gooseberry and strawberry jam

1½ LB. GOOSEBERRIES   ¼ PINT WATER
1½ LB. STRAWBERRIES   3 LB. SUGAR

Top and tail the gooseberries and hull the strawberries. Put the gooseberries into a preserving pan with water and simmer until tender. Add the strawberries and cook for a further 3-4 minutes. Add sugar and cook over a low heat until dissolved, then boil rapidly until setting point is reached. Skim, pour into hot sterilized jars and cover tightly. **Yields about 5 lb.**

General hints on making jellies

Most of the same rules apply as for jam-making, but the method requires the use of a jelly bag. The stages are as follows:

1. Clean the fruit but do not prepare as for jam. For instance, there is no need to peel or core apples. Place in the pan with the recommended amount of water, which varies considerably according to the type of fruit. Simmer gently until tender. This may take up to an hour.

2. When the fruit is cooked, turn the contents of the pan into a jelly bag, set up to drip over a basin, first scalding the bag by pouring boiling water through it. A proper jelly bag is made of a closely woven calico or flannel, so that only the juice drips through. Even a trace of pulp will turn the jelly cloudy. If you have no jelly bag, make one from a square of suitable material, either 18 inches or 24 inches square. Machine two adjacent sides together to make a triangular pocket, making sure the tip is well joined. Attach 4 pieces of tape evenly spaced round the top.

3. Hang the jelly bag over a bowl large enough to take the juice that will drip through, by attaching the tapes to the 4 legs of an upturned chair on the kitchen table. If you have no jelly bag, you can improvise one as shown in the drawing below. Use several

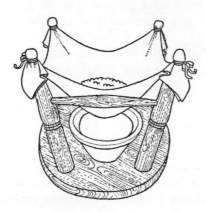

thicknesses of muslin, tying them with tape or string to the chair legs as shown, and allow a generous pocket for the fruit pulp. Sterilize with boiling water as for a jelly bag.

4. Allow the juice to drain through completely, but do not disturb or squeeze the bag, as this makes the jelly cloudy. If liked, leave to drip overnight, but never longer than 24 hours. When using fruits such as currants, apples or gooseberries, which set well, you can boil up the fruit a second time with half the original quantity of water and allow to strain again. The two liquids should then be mixed.

5. Measure the quantity of liquid, and reheat in the preserving pan. Add the sugar, allowing 1 lb. sugar to each pint of liquid in most cases, and allow the sugar to dissolve. Bring to the boil then proceed as for making jam.

6. Fill the jars while the jelly is still very hot, or it may begin to set in the pan.

Note : All these jellies can be served with hot savoury dishes.

Redcurrant jelly

4 LB. REDCURRANTS   SUGAR
2 PINTS WATER

Put the prepared redcurrants into a preserving pan or saucepan with the water. Cook until soft, about 30 minutes. Put into a jelly bag and leave to strain overnight. Measure the liquid, transfer to a preserving pan and add 1 lb. sugar to every pint of liquid. Dissolve the sugar over a low heat, then bring to the boil and boil rapidly until setting point is reached, about 10 minutes. Skim, pour into hot sterilized jars and cover tightly. **Yields about 4 lb.**

Variation : Cranberry jelly can be made in the same way, using the same proportions, or very slightly less water.

Bramble jelly

2 LB. BLACKBERRIES $\frac{1}{4}$ PINT WATER
2 MEDIUM COOKING APPLES   SUGAR

Wash and cut up the apples, but do not peel or core (the core and pips help the jelly to set). Wash the blackberries. Put the apples and blackberries together into a preserving pan, add the water, and simmer until soft. Put into a jelly bag and leave to strain overnight. Measure juice and allow 1 lb. sugar to each pint of juice. Cook over a low heat until sugar has dissolved, then boil rapidly until setting point is reached. Skim, pour into hot sterilized jars and cover tightly. **Yields about 3 lb.**

Apple geranium jelly

4 LB. COOKING APPLES	2 PINTS WATER
12 GERANIUM LEAVES	SUGAR

Wash and cut up the apples, but do not peel or core. Wash the geranium leaves, removing any part that is imperfect. Put the apple and geranium leaves into a preserving pan, add the water, and simmer to a pulp. Put into a jelly bag and leave to strain overnight. Measure juice and allow 1 lb. sugar to each pint of juice. Cook over a low heat until sugar has dissolved, then boil rapidly until setting point is reached. Skim, pour into hot sterilized jars and cover tightly. **Yields about 4 lb.**

Sloe and apple jelly

4 LB. COOKING APPLES	ABOUT 2 PINTS WATER
2 LB. SLOES	SUGAR

Wash and cut up the apples, but do not peel or core. Put into a preserving pan with the sloes, just cover with water and simmer to a pulp. Put into a jelly bag and leave to strain overnight. Measure juice and allow 1 lb. sugar to each pint of juice. Cook over a low heat until sugar has dissolved, then boil rapidly until setting point is reached. Skim, pour into hot sterilized jars and cover tightly. **Yields about 6 lb.**

Mint jelly

2 LB. GREEN COOKING APPLES	2 TABLESPOONS LEMON JUICE
BUNCH OF MINT	GRANULATED SUGAR
2 PINTS WATER	FEW DROPS GREEN COLOURING

Wash and quarter apples, but do not peel or core them. Wash mint thoroughly. Put half the mint and the apples into a preserving pan or large saucepan with the water and lemon juice and cook until a thick pulp. Put into a jelly bag and leave to

45

strain overnight. Measure the liquid and add 1 lb. sugar to every pint of liquid. Chop the remaining mint and add. Put over a gentle heat until the sugar has dissolved, then boil rapidly until setting point is reached, about 10 minutes. Add green food colouring, pour into hot sterilized jars and cover tightly. **Yields about 3 lb.**

Haw jelly

3 LB. HAWS	LEMONS
3 PINTS WATER	SUGAR

Wash the haws well and put into a preserving pan with water. Simmer for about 1 hour. Put into a jelly bag and leave to strain overnight. Measure the juice and allow juice of 1 lemon and 1 lb. sugar to each pint of juice. Put over a low heat until sugar has dissolved, then boil rapidly until setting point is reached. Pour into hot sterilized jars and cover tightly. **Yields about 6 lb.**

Medlar jelly

1 LB. MEDLARS	SUGAR
¼ PINT WATER	LEMON

Put the washed fruit into a preserving pan or saucepan with the water and cook until soft. Put into a jelly bag and leave to strain overnight. Measure the liquid, transfer to a preserving pan, and add 1 lb. sugar and juice of half a lemon to every pint of liquid. Dissolve sugar over a low heat, then bring to the boil and boil rapidly until setting point is reached. Skim, pour into hot sterilized jars and cover. **Yields about 1½ lb.**

Cucumber jelly

ABOUT 4 LB. CUCUMBERS	LEMONS
4 TABLESPOONS WATER	GROUND GINGER
SUGAR	

Wash the cucumbers, cut up and put into a preserving pan with the water. Simmer until a soft pulp. Put into a jelly bag and leave to strain overnight. Measure the juice and allow 1 lb. sugar, the juice of 1 lemon and a pinch of ginger to each pint of juice. Put over a low heat until the sugar has dissolved, then boil rapidly until setting point is reached. Pour into hot sterilized jars and cover tightly. **Yields about 2½ lb.**

Parsley honey

This is a good recipe to make use of parsley that has gone to seed. Pack a large enamel or stainless steel saucepan full of wet, washed parsley, and add just enough water to come through, but not cover. Bring to the boil, and simmer for 30 minutes. Strain the liquor through a jelly bag. Measure, and for every pint of liquid add 1 lb. of sugar. Bring slowly to the boil, then boil very rapidly until it begins to set. Pour into clean warm jars, and cover as for fruit jellies. The consistency should be that of thin honey.

General hints on making marmalades

Although the process is much the same as for making jams and jellies, there are two essential differences.
1. The peel of citrus fruits, which gives much of the bulk and flavour, takes some time to prepare and longer cooking to soften it before the sugar can be added.
2. The setting agent, pectin, is largely present in the pith and pips rather than the flesh or juice of the fruit. These should therefore not be discarded, but carefully gathered and tied loosely in a square of muslin. If the muslin bag is attached to the handle of the pan and allowed to hang down inside during the first boiling, it can easily be removed at the stage of adding the sugar, and thrown away.

The best oranges to make a classic marmalade are Seville bitter

oranges, but other bitter oranges can be used. Sweet oranges, unless mixed with some bitter oranges or other citrus fruit, will not give a palatable result. The fruit should be used when only just ripe, so it is wise to order it in advance from the greengrocer, and collect as soon as it is delivered, as it is hard for the housewife to judge when citrus fruit becomes over-ripe.

Some recipes suggest halving and squeezing the fruit first, then separating the pith from the peel and shredding the peel. Others suggest skinning the fruit, separating the flesh from the pith, and adding the chopped flesh to the shredded peel. Whichever method is followed, the white pith and pips are intended only to be used to extract their pectin content, and the finished marmalade should contain only the peel and juice, or peel and flesh, of the fruit. To skin fruit easily, soak them first in boiling water for 1 or 2 minutes.

The prepared fruit is often placed with the water and left to soak for 24 hours or at least overnight. This tends to soften the peel and reduce the cooking time. It is quicker to mince the peel than to shred it, but this gives rather a coarse cut.

To make marmalade: Bring the fruit and water mixture to the boil, cook gently until quite tender, at least 1 hour, and the mixture is reduced by at least one third. Remove the muslin bag of pith and pips, add the sugar, allowing 1 lb. to each pint of liquid, allow to dissolve over gentle heat, then boil rapidly for about 20 minutes or until setting point is reached.

To pot marmalade: Remove scum immediately, as if it subsides on the peel it is difficult to remove. Allow to cool slightly, then stir to distribute the peel evenly. (Do not stir clear jelly marmalades.) Pour into hot sterilized jars, and immediately cover with waxed paper circles. Cover in the usual way when cold.

Making jams, jellies and marmalades in a pressure cooker

A pressure cooker can be extremely useful for making preserves, particularly marmalade, as the peel will be softened in about 15 minutes, instead of the usual 2 hours. However, the pressure cooker is only really suitable for jams and jellies in which the fruit takes some time to cook, e.g. jams made from dried fruit, plum jam and gooseberry jam, and it is not advisable to use it for such quick cooking jams as raspberry and strawberry. For softening, the fruit should be put into the pressure cooker with the water, brought up to 15 lb. pressure and cooked for the required length of time. As a simple guide, reduce the usual quantity of water to half and quarter the cooking time. Before the sugar is added the pressure must be returned to room temperature and the jam is then made in the usual way. It is *most important* that the jam should not be cooked under pressure once the sugar is added under any circumstances. Also, do remember that the pan should not be more than half full.

Old English marmalade

2 LB. SEVILLE ORANGES	6 LB. GRANULATED SUGAR
1 LEMON	2 TABLESPOONS BLACK TREACLE
7 PINTS WATER	

Wash the fruit, cut in half and squeeze out juice. Remove as much of the pith as possible and put in a muslin bag with the pips. Shred the peel. Put the peel into a preserving pan with the juice, water and muslin bag. Bring to the boil and simmer gently for about 2 hours or until the peel is tender and the liquid is reduced by half. Remove the bag of pips, squeezing gently to extract as much pectin as possible. Add the sugar and treacle and heat gently until the sugar has dissolved. Bring to the boil and boil rapidly until setting point is reached. Remove from heat and allow to stand for 5–10 minutes so that the peel becomes evenly distributed. Pour into hot sterilized jars and cover tightly. **Yields about 9 lb.**

Clear orange marmalade

3 LB. SEVILLE ORANGES	6 PINTS WATER
2 LEMONS	4 LB. GRANULATED SUGAR
1 SWEET ORANGE	

Wash the fruit, cut in half and squeeze out the juice, reserving the pulp and pips. Scrape all the white pith away from the skins. Put the pith, pips and pulp into a bowl with 2 pints of water. Shred the peel finely and place in another bowl with 4 pints of water, and the juice. Leave both to stand overnight. Strain the pips, etc., through a muslin bag and tie it loosely. Put the strained liquor, bag, peel and juice all together in a preserving pan, simmer until the peel is tender. Remove from heat and discard the muslin bag without squeezing. Add the sugar, allow to dissolve completely over gentle heat, then boil rapidly until setting point is reached. Remove from the heat, cool for a few minutes, then pot and cover tightly. **Yields about 10 lb.**

Three fruit marmalade

1 GRAPEFRUIT	3 PINTS WATER
2 LEMONS	3 LB. SUGAR
1 SWEET ORANGE	

Wash the fruit and cut in half. Squeeze out the juice and tie the pips and pith in a muslin bag. Shred the peel finely and put into a preserving pan with water and muslin bag. Leave to soak overnight. The following day simmer gently for about 1½ hours or until the contents of the pan are reduced to about one third. Remove muslin bag, squeezing gently to extract as much pectin as possible. Stir in the sugar and cook over a low heat until dissolved, then boil rapidly until setting point is reached. Leave to cool for about 10 minutes so that the peel is evenly distributed, then pour into hot sterilized jars. Cover tightly. **Yields about 5 lb.**

Minced peel marmalade

3 LB. SEVILLE ORANGES	4 LB. GRANULATED SUGAR
JUICE OF 2 LEMONS	2 LB. DARK BROWN SUGAR
6 PINTS WATER	KNOB OF BUTTER

Wash the fruit and cut in half. Squeeze juice and tie the pips in a muslin bag. Mince peel coarsely. Put minced peel, lemon juice, water and muslin bag into a preserving pan. Simmer the mixture gently for about 2 hours or until the peel is tender and the contents of the saucepan are reduced to about half. Remove the bag of pips, squeezing gently to remove as much pectin as possible. Stir in the sugar and cook over a low heat until the sugar is dissolved. Bring to the boil and boil rapidly until setting point is reached. Remove from the heat and stir in the butter; this helps to reduce the scum. Leave to cool for about 10 minutes so that the peel is evenly distributed, then pour into hot sterilized jars and cover tightly. **Yields about 10 lb.**

3

Pickles, chutneys and sauces

L ate summer and autumn are the traditional times for making
pickles, chutneys and sauces. Gardens and orchards are full
of vegetables and fruit, and the produce is at its best and cheapest.
For the farmer's wife, it probably costs no more than the trouble
of persuading the children to help with the picking.

Fruit, vegetables, herbs, spices and vinegar form the basis of
most pickles and chutneys, and the vinegar acts as a preservative,
preventing deterioration. It should always be boiled before use, as
this helps the preserve to keep longer.

Making pickles: The chosen vegetables are usually put into either
a wet or dry brine, left overnight or for several days to mature,
and then packed into a jar with the vinegar.

Making chutneys: All the ingredients are generally simmered
together for several hours until they form a thick pulp, and the
mixture is then bottled and sealed.

Making sauces: For long keeping they should really be sterilized.
In all cases, the jars themselves should be sterilized before potting,
and must therefore be strong enough to withstand heat. The corks
should also be boiled at the same time, or covered with clean
greaseproof paper.

To sterilize jars and bottles: Put carefully into a pan of cold
water so that they fill completely and bring up to the boil. Lift out
on to a wooden board. (Do not put on a cold surface or glass may
crack.) Kitchen tongs are useful for this purpose.

51

To sterilize sauces: Pour boiling sauce into the hot sterilized jar, cork lightly, and stand jars in a pan of boiling water padded with corrugated paper or a folded tea towel in the base, and boil steadily for 10 minutes. Take care bottles do not overbalance. If necessary, lightly tie corks on with string to prevent them from being blown off. Remove from the heat, transfer jars to a wooden board and cork firmly.

Suitable equipment for storing: Old jars and bottles can certainly be re-used, provided metal lids are not allowed to come into contact with the preservative. Glass or stone jars are best, but ordinary jam jars can be used, covered with two layers of grease-proof or waxed paper, and then with kitchen foil tied down securely.

To coat seals with wax: This process is useful for sealing narrow necked bottles. Have melted candle or paraffin wax ready, and brush round the cork immediately to make an airtight seal. Or dip the corks of small bottles quickly into the melted wax past the level of the seal. If necessary repeat with a second layer of wax, then cover with moulded kitchen foil.

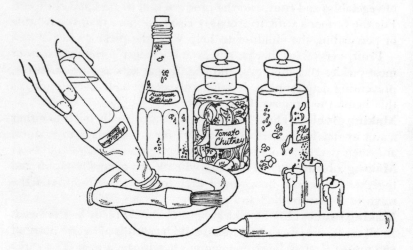

Sealing with metal bottle tops: A small circle of waxed paper can be put over the sauce in the bottle immediately after sterilization, then a teaspoon of melted wax poured over the top. Cover with an ordinary metal bottle top, which must fit exactly. The same method can be used for bottles with a screw top lids.

It is most important when making pickles, chutneys and sauces that an aluminium, enamelled or stainless steel pan should be used; on no account must a brass, copper or iron pan be used as the acid in the vinegar will eat into the metal, giving the preserve a strong metallic taste. Always use a wooden spoon for mixing or stirring. For the same reason, any sieving should be done with a hair or nylon sieve, and it is unwise to use a metal one.

Vinegar based preserves must be well covered to prevent evaporation of the vinegar and for this reason ordinary jam covers are not suitable. Jars with ground glass stoppers are ideal and before sealing, the rim of the stopper should be smeared with a little vaseline to make sure it is airtight. Corks are another excellent method of sealing and again should either be smeared with a little vaseline or a layer of vinegar-proof paper (such as parchment paper) put between the container and the cork. A very good way of storing is to cover the preserve with melted paraffin wax. This forms a synthetic skin through which vinegar cannot escape, and can be bought quite cheaply from many chemists. Alternatively the preserve can be covered with several thicknesses of vinegar-proof paper.

It is advisable to store pickles, chutneys and sauces in a cool, dry place which preferably should be dark as well. Apart from their use for serving with cold and hot meals and salad, chutneys and sauces are also excellent in stews, casseroles, meat loaves and curries and can be used in countless other ways to flavour made-up dishes.

Wine, malt and spiced vinegar

Vinegar is a necessary ingredient for most of the following recipes. Buy good bottled vinegar, with an acetic acid content of at least 5 per cent. The acetic acid content of cheap barrelled vinegar is often too low to keep pickled vegetables well. White vinegar is preferable if appearance is important, as when preparing pickles for show purposes, but malt vinegar gives a richer flavour. Pickles made with unboiled vinegar will not keep long, so vinegar must be boiled at some point in either the spicing or cooking processes.

To make spiced vinegar: To each quart of vinegar add $\frac{1}{2}$ oz. cloves, $\frac{1}{2}$ oz. ginger, $\frac{1}{2}$ oz. cinnamon, $\frac{1}{2}$ oz. allspice and $\frac{1}{2}$ oz. white pepper. Use whole spices, not the ground variety. Put all together in a well corked bottle and allow to steep for at least 4 weeks or longer. Shake the bottle each week. Taste the vinegar and if spicy enough, strain off the spices and recork the bottle until required. Or tie 1 oz. mixed pickling spice in a piece of muslin and put into a saucepan with 2 pints of vinegar. Bring slowly to the boil, remove from the heat, cover and leave for 2 hours. Remove the spice bag. Spiced vinegar is used for a large number of pickles and chutneys.

Pickled hard boiled eggs

2 DOZEN EGGS   3 PINTS SPICED VINEGAR

Hard boil the eggs for 12 minutes. Remove from the heat and place under running water to cool quickly. Shell the eggs, place in wide-necked jars; strain the spiced vinegar over them. Seal and leave for at least 2 weeks before eating.

Spiced pickled peaches

4 LB. GRANULATED SUGAR $\frac{1}{2}$ OZ. ALLSPICE
2 PINTS DISTILLED MALT $\frac{1}{4}$ OZ. ROOT GINGER
  VINEGAR   1 CINNAMON STICK, BROKEN
THINLY PEELED ZEST 1 LEMON   IN PIECES
$\frac{1}{2}$ OZ. CLOVES   8 LB. FIRM PEACHES

Put the sugar into a preserving pan or large saucepan with the vinegar and leave to dissolve over a low heat. Tie the lemon zest, cloves, allspice, ginger and cinnamon in a muslin bag and add to the pan. Peel peaches, cut in half and remove stones. Put the prepared peaches into a weak salt and water solution to prevent them from browning. When they are all prepared, rinse in cold water and add to the pan. Cover and simmer gently for 20–30 minutes until tender. Do not cook too quickly or the peaches will break up. When the peaches are tender, remove carefully with a draining spoon and arrange neatly in jars. Boil the liquid rapidly for about 5 minutes until it is the consistency of thin syrup. Pour over the peaches while still hot. Cover and leave to mature for at least 3 months before using. **Yields about 8 lb.**

Pickled orange wedges

4 LARGE ORANGES   3 INCH STICK CINNAMON
$\frac{1}{2}$ TEASPOON BICARBONATE OF   1 OZ. ROOT GINGER, BRUISED
  SODA   1 PINT VINEGAR
$\frac{1}{2}$ OZ. WHOLE ALLSPICE   1 LB. GRANULATED SUGAR
12 CLOVES

Wash the oranges and cut each orange into about 8 segments, leaving the peel on. Cover with water, add bicarbonate of soda, bring to the boil and simmer for 20 minutes. Tie the spices in a piece of muslin, put in a saucepan with the vinegar, cover and simmer for about 20 minutes. When the orange peel is soft, drain off water. Remove the spice bag from the vinegar. Add sugar and keep over a low heat until the sugar has dissolved. Bring to the boil, add the orange segments and simmer, covered, for a further 20 minutes. Remove the orange segments with a draining spoon and pack into jars. Boil the vinegar and sugar until the consistency of thin syrup and pour over the oranges. Seal. **Yields about 2 lb.**

Pickled artichokes

JERUSALEM ARTICHOKES   WATER
SALT   SPICED VINEGAR

Clean and peel the artichokes and cook for about 10 minutes in a weak brine solution (allowing 1 oz. salt to $1\frac{1}{2}$ pints water). When cold, pack into wide necked jars and cover with hot spiced vinegar. Seal.

Pickled red cabbage

4 LB. RED CABBAGE   4 PINTS SPICED VINEGAR
4 OZ. COOKING SALT

Discard outer leaves from the cabbage and shred heart finely. Separate shreds, place the cabbage on a large dish or tray and sprinkle with salt. Leave overnight. The next day, drain off the liquid salt and pack the cabbage into jars. Cover with the cold spiced vinegar. Seal and leave for 2 weeks before using. **Yields 4 lb.**

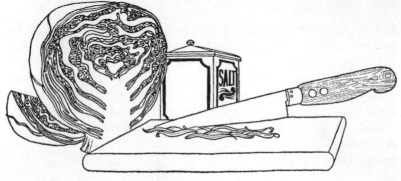

Pickled nasturtium seeds

NASTURTIUM SEEDS	6 PEPPERCORNS
1 PINT VINEGAR	1 TEASPOON SALT
2 BAY LEAVES	

Pick the seeds before they fall and either dry on a tray in the sun or in a very cool oven. Put the vinegar with bay leaves, peppercorns and salt into a pan and bring to the boil. Remove from the heat and leave to go cold. Pack the seeds into sterilized bottles, cover with strained vinegar. Seal and keep for at least 1 month before using.

Pickled mushrooms

1 LB. BUTTON MUSHROOMS	1 TEASPOON SALT
1 SMALL ONION	$\frac{1}{2}$ TEASPOON WHITE PEPPER
1 PINT DISTILLED MALT	$\frac{1}{4}$ OZ. ROOT GINGER
VINEGAR	

Clean the mushrooms by wiping with a damp cloth dipped in salt; it is not necessary to peel them. Put into a pan. Peel and slice the onion and put in the pan with remaining ingredients. Simmer until the mushrooms are tender. Remove the mushrooms with a draining spoon, put into a jar. Cover with strained hot vinegar and seal. **Yields 1 lb.**

Mixed pickles

8 OZ. COOKING SALT	8 OZ. SMALL RIDGE
3 PINTS WATER	CUCUMBERS
1 SMALL FIRM CAULIFLOWER	8 OZ. FRENCH BEANS
8 OZ. PICKLING ONIONS	2–3 PINTS SPICED VINEGAR
8 OZ. GREEN TOMATOES	

Put the salt and water into a pan, bring to the boil and allow to become cold before using. Break the cauliflower into sprigs; peel the onions; cut the unpeeled cucumbers into cubes; quarter the tomatoes and top and tail the beans. Put all the ingredients into a bowl, pour over the prepared brine and leave for 24 hours. Drain, pack closely in jars and cover with the cold spiced vinegar. Allow the vinegar to seep through all the vegetables and top up if necessary. Seal and leave to mature for at least 1 month before using. **Yields 3–4 lb.**

Note : Allow plenty of vinegar above the surface of the vegetables. They expand as they absorb the vinegar.

Pickled bilberries

3 LB. BILBERRIES	3–4 CLOVES
I PINT VINEGAR	BLADE MACE
4 OZ. SOFT BROWN SUGAR	I INCH STICK CINNAMON
¼ OZ. ALLSPICE	2 TEASPOONS GRATED
¼ OZ. PEPPERCORNS	HORSERADISH

Discard any blemished berries and pack the sound ones into a large pickle jar. Put all the remaining ingredients into a saucepan, bring slowly to the boil and simmer gently for 10–15 minutes. Strain over the bilberries. Cover the jar with a plate, putting a weight on top to keep the fruit down if necessary. After 3 days pour off the liquid and reboil it. Pour it on to the berries while hot. Seal the jar when the contents are cold. **Yields about 3 lb.**

Pickled shallots

SHALLOTS	WATER
SALT	SPICED VINEGAR

Rub off the outer skins but do not peel the shallots. Immerse in a brine solution, using ½ lb. salt to 4 pints water. Leave overnight. Remove from the brine and peel, using a stainless steel knife, or they may discolour. Cover with fresh brine, and leave for a further 24 hours. Drain thoroughly and pack tightly into jars. Cover with cold spiced vinegar, making sure the vinegar comes at least ½ inch above the shallots. Allow to mature for 3 months before using. They are delicious with cheese or cold meats.

Pickled walnuts

WALNUTS	SALT
WATER	SPICED VINEGAR

Walnuts for pickling must be young, green and easily pierced with a fork. Prick walnuts all over (it is advisable to use gloves when doing this as they stain badly) and put into a brine solution made with 1 lb. salt to 2 pints water. Leave for 9 days, changing the brine every 3 days. Drain walnuts, spread on a tray and leave exposed to the air until they are quite black. Pack into a jar and cover with the cold spiced vinegar. After a couple of days, top up the vinegar and seal. Leave for 1 month before using.

Green tomato chutney

2 LB. GREEN TOMATOES
3 PINTS DISTILLED MALT
   VINEGAR
3 LARGE COOKING APPLES
2 LB. ONIONS
1 LB. STONED RAISINS

1 LB. 6 OZ. DEMERARA SUGAR
1 TABLESPOON SALT
1 TEASPOON CAYENNE PEPPER
2 OZ. DRIED ROOT GINGER
$1\frac{1}{2}$ OZ. MUSTARD SEED

Chop the tomatoes, put into a pan with half the vinegar and simmer until soft. Sieve. Peel, core and chop the apples, peel and chop the onions and chop raisins. Return purée to the pan with the apples, onions, raisins, sugar, salt, cayenne pepper and remaining vinegar. Tie the ginger and mustard seed in a muslin bag and add to the pan. Simmer until the chutney is thick, about 1 hour. Remove the spice bag, pour into hot sterilized jars and seal. **Yields about 6 lb.**

Rhubarb chutney

5 LB. RHUBARB
1 LB. ONIONS
2 LB. SOFT BROWN SUGAR
$\frac{1}{2}$ OZ. GROUND GINGER

$\frac{1}{2}$ OZ. SALT
$\frac{1}{2}$ OZ. CURRY POWDER
$1\frac{1}{2}$ PINTS VINEGAR

Chop the rhubarb, and peel and finely chop the onions. Put into a preserving pan or large saucepan with the sugar, ginger, salt, curry powder and half the vinegar. Cook until tender. Add the remaining vinegar and cook until thick, about $1\frac{1}{2}$ hours. Pour into hot sterilized jars and seal. Leave for about 1 month before using. **Yields about 6 lb.**

Plum chutney

2 LB. PLUMS

1 LB. CARROTS

3 CLOVES GARLIC

1 PINT VINEGAR

1 LB. SOFT BROWN SUGAR

$\frac{1}{2}$ TEASPOON CAYENNE PEPPER

2 OZ. SALT

$\frac{1}{2}$ OZ. GROUND GINGER

1 LB. COOKING DATES

Remove the stones from the plums and chop. Crack a few of the stones and remove the kernels. Clean and grate the carrots, peel and finely chop or crush the garlic. Put the plums, kernels, carrots, garlic and vinegar in a pan and simmer until soft, about 50 minutes. Add the sugar, cayenne pepper, salt, ginger and chopped dates and boil for about 30 minutes or until thick. Pour into hot sterilized jars and seal. **Yields 3–3$\frac{1}{2}$ lb.**

Turnip chutney

2 LB. TURNIPS

1 LB. APPLES

1 LB. ONIONS

$\frac{1}{2}$ OZ. TURMERIC

1 TEASPOON DRY MUSTARD

2 PINTS VINEGAR

8 OZ. SULTANAS

8 OZ. SOFT BROWN SUGAR

$\frac{1}{4}$ TEASPOON GROUND BLACK PEPPER

2 OZ. SALT

Wash the turnips, quarter and cook in boiling water until soft. Drain and mash well. Peel, core and chop the apples and peel and chop the onions. Mix turmeric and mustard with a little of the vinegar. Put all the ingredients into a preserving pan and simmer gently until thick, about 1 hour. Pour into hot sterilized jars and seal. **Yields about 5 lb.**

Plum and apple chutney

3 LB. PLUMS	1 TEASPOON GROUND CLOVES
1 LB. APPLES	1 TEASPOON POWDERED
1 LB. ONIONS	CINNAMON
1 LB. STONED RAISINS	1 TEASPOON GROUND GINGER
1 LB. SUGAR	1 TEASPOON GROUND ALLSPICE
2 OZ. SALT	1 PINT VINEGAR

Stone the plums and roughly chop. Peel, core and chop the apples and peel and chop the onions. Chop the raisins. Put all the ingredients into a preserving pan or large saucepan and simmer gently until thick, about $1\frac{1}{2}$ hours. Pour into hot sterilized jars and seal. Leave for about 2 months before using. **Yields about 5 lb.**

Apple and tomato chutney

2 LB. COOKING APPLES	1 PINT VINEGAR
2 LB. ONIONS	1 LB. BLACK TREACLE
2 LB. RIPE TOMATOES	2 TEASPOONS SALT
$\frac{1}{2}$ OZ. MIXED PICKLING SPICE	3 OZ. MUSTARD SEEDS OR
8 OZ. SULTANAS	1 OZ. DRY MUSTARD

Peel and core the apples and chop. Peel and chop the onions. Skin and chop the tomatoes. Tie the pickling spice in a muslin bag. Put all the ingredients into a pan and simmer for $2\frac{1}{4}$–$2\frac{1}{2}$ hours or until thick. Remove the pickling spice, pour into hot sterilized jars and seal. **Yields about 6 lb.**

Marrow chutney

5 LB. MARROW	8 OZ. CURRANTS
2 OZ. SALT	8 OZ. SOFT BROWN SUGAR
8 OZ. ONIONS	$\frac{1}{2}$ OZ. GROUND GINGER
8 OZ. STONED RAISINS	1 OZ. MUSTARD SEED
8 OZ. SULTANAS	1 PINT VINEGAR

Peel the marrow, remove seeds and cut into small cubes. Put into a bowl, sprinkling salt between the layers, and leave for 24 hours. Peel and chop the onions and cook in a very little water until tender. Add all the ingredients except the marrow and bring to the boil. Drain and wash the marrow and add to the pan. Simmer gently until the mixture is thick, about 2 hours. Pour into hot

sterilized jars and seal. Leave for about 2 months before using.
Yields about 6 lb.

Orange chutney

4 ORANGES	4 LB. SOFT BROWN SUGAR
2 APPLES	I OZ. SEEDLESS RAISINS
I ONION	I PINT VINEGAR
4 OZ. PRESERVED STEM	I OZ. SALT
GINGER	$\frac{1}{4}$ TEASPOON PEPPER
$\frac{1}{2}$ OZ. CHILLIES	

Peel the oranges, removing all the white pith and pips, and chop.
Peel, core and chop the apples and peel and chop the onion.
Chop the ginger and chillies. Put all the ingredients into a pan
and simmer gently until thick, about 1 hour. Pour into hot sterilized jars and seal. **Yields about 4 lb.**

Gooseberry chutney

3 LB. HARD GOOSEBERRIES	I PINT MALT VINEGAR
3 MEDIUM SIZE ONIONS	$\frac{1}{2}$ PINT WHITE WINE VINEGAR
2 TEASPOONS DRY MUSTARD	8 OZ. SULTANAS
I TEASPOON TURMERIC	12 OZ. SOFT BROWN SUGAR
I TEASPOON GROUND GINGER	2 TEASPOONS SALT

Top and tail the gooseberries and wash. Coarsely mince with the
peeled onions. Mix the mustard, turmeric and ginger with a little
of the vinegar and put into a pan with all other ingredients. Cook
over a gentle heat until the mixture is thick, about 2 hours. Turn
into hot sterilized jars and seal. Keep for at least 1 month before
using. **Yields about 3 lb.**

Raspberry relish

I QUART RIPE RASPBERRIES	$\frac{1}{2}$ TEASPOON DRY MUSTARD
$\frac{1}{2}$ PINT WHITE WINE VINEGAR	$\frac{1}{2}$ TEASPOON MIXED SPICE
$\frac{1}{2}$ TEASPOON SALT	SUGAR

Put the raspberries with the vinegar into a preserving pan and
simmer until the fruit is a pulp. Strain, and press all the pulp
except the seeds back into the pan. Add the salt, mustard and

61

the mixed spice. Simmer gently for 20 minutes, then strain again. Add 6 oz. granulated sugar to each pint of liquid, allow sugar to dissolve over moderate heat, then boil quickly until thick. Pour into hot sterilized jar, seal. Serve with any cold cooked meat. **Yields about 3 lb.**

Sweet piccalilli

1 MEDIUM SIZE MARROW	$\frac{1}{2}$ OZ. TURMERIC
1 CAULIFLOWER	$\frac{1}{4}$ OZ. GROUND GINGER
1 CUCUMBER	$\frac{1}{2}$ OZ. GROUND NUTMEG
1 LB. YOUNG FRENCH BEANS	10 OZ. GRANULATED SUGAR
2 OZ. SALT	2 OZ. FLOUR
2 OZ. DRY MUSTARD	2 PINTS VINEGAR

Chop the vegetables into $\frac{1}{2}$–1 inch chunks. Sprinkle with half the salt, cover with water and soak overnight, then drain off water. Mix all the dry ingredients with a little of the vinegar to make a smooth paste. Add remainder of the vinegar to the vegetables and simmer in a strong pan until barely tender, about 10 minutes. Add some boiling vinegar to the smoothly blended paste. Return to the pan and boil for 10 minutes, stirring all the time, and allow to thicken. Turn into hot sterilized jars and seal. **Yields about 9 lb.**

Tomato sauce

9 LB. TOMATOES
1 LB. ONIONS
6 CLOVES GARLIC
½ PINT DISTILLED MALT
  VINEGAR
1 OZ. DRY MUSTARD

1½ OZ. SALT
1 TEASPOON MIXED SPICE
½ TEASPOON CAYENNE PEPPER
1 TEASPOON PAPRIKA
1½ LB. GRANULATED SUGAR

Skin the tomatoes and chop coarsely. Peel and finely chop onions and crush garlic. Put into a preserving pan or large saucepan and simmer for about 15 minutes. Add vinegar, mustard, salt, mixed spice, cayenne and paprika, mix well and simmer for about 1 hour. Add sugar and heat gently until dissolved, then boil gently for a further 15 minutes. Pour into hot sterilized jars and seal. **Yields about 7 lb.**

Tomato relish

1 LB. TOMATOES
2 GREEN PEPPERS
1 LB. ONIONS
2 CLOVES GARLIC
1 LB. COOKING APPLES
½ PINT DISTILLED MALT
  VINEGAR

12 OZ. GRANULATED SUGAR
1 TABLESPOON SALT
1 TABLESPOON PAPRIKA
½ TEASPOON CAYENNE PEPPER
1 TABLESPOON MADE MUSTARD
½ TEASPOON MIXED SPICE
5 OZ. CAN TOMATO PURÉE

Skin the tomatoes and chop. Cut the peppers in half, remove core and seeds and chop finely. Peel and chop the onions and crush the garlic. Peel, core and finely chop the apples. Put all prepared ingredients into a pan with the vinegar, cover and simmer for about 30 minutes, stirring occasionally or until all ingredients are tender. Add remaining ingredients, bring to the boil and boil for about 5 minutes, stirring frequently until fairly thick. Pour into hot sterilized jars and seal. **Yields about 4½ lb.**

Nasturtium sauce

8 SHALLOTS
2 PINTS VINEGAR
6 CLOVES
1 TEASPOON SALT

½ TEASPOON CAYENNE PEPPER
2 PINTS PRESSED NASTURTIUM
  FLOWERS
1 TEASPOON SOY SAUCE

63

Bruise the shallots and put into a pan with the vinegar, cloves, salt and cayenne pepper. Simmer for 10 minutes, then pour over the flowers. Cover closely for 2 months. Strain the mixture, and add the soy sauce and pour into hot sterilized bottles. Seal. **Yields about 2 pints.**

Spiced cranberry sauce

I LB. CRANBERRIES	I TEASPOON MIXED SPICE
¼ PINT MALT OR WHITE WINE	8 OZ. SUGAR
VINEGAR	½ TEASPOON SALT

Wash the berries and put into a saucepan with the vinegar. Cook gently until reduced to a pulp. Sieve and return to the pan with the spice, sugar and salt. Cook, stirring over a low heat until the mixture is thick. Turn into hot sterilized bottles and seal. **Yields about 1 pint.**

Mint sauce for storing

8 OZ. MINT LEAVES	12 OZ. GRANULATED SUGAR
I PINT VINEGAR	PINCH BORAX POWDER

Wash, dry and finely chop the mint. Put the vinegar, sugar and borax into a pan and heat gently until the sugar dissolves. Half fill bottles with the mint and top up with the cooled vinegar. Seal. The bottles must either have screw tops or very tightly fitting corks. To make sure that they are airtight, dip the necks of the bottles in melted paraffin wax.

Mushroom ketchup

3 LB. MUSHROOMS	½ PINT SPICED VINEGAR
3 OZ. SALT	2 TEASPOONS CHOPPED ONION

Mince or chop the mushrooms, sprinkle with salt and leave for 24–36 hours. Add the vinegar and the onion to the mushrooms and their liquor and simmer gently for 2½ hours. Strain through muslin into hot sterilized jars. Seal. **Yields about 3 lb.**

4

Bottling and canning
fresh produce

The principal of preserving by sterilizing and excluding bacteria-laden air from the bottles has only recently been understood, which explains why salting and smoking far preceded this process in the farmhouse kitchen. Even the making of jam and other sweet preserves is a less venerable art than either wine-making or meat curing, mainly because sugar was once only readily available in the form of honey; and this is why every farmhouse, and indeed almost every hovel, kept a few skeps of bees. Sugar cane was first known in Europe in the seventh century, and by the time this country had emerged from the dark ages into the medieval era of good husbandry and more luxurious eating, it was beginning to be imported. The returning Crusaders introduced sugar from the East. However it was a rare and expensive commodity, although the sugar cane industry flourished under the Portuguese in Madeira from the early fifteenth century, and in the New World from about a hundred years later. Beet sugar, on which we now greatly depend, was a failure here in the early 1830s, and in fact only succeeded in 1912, in time to be of great service to us in the two world wars.

There was a time when bottling fruit and vegetables was looked upon by urban housewives as a mysterious art, understood and practised only by the farmer's wife. Canning was then entirely a commercial process and of course housewives were coming to rely more and more on canned peas and plums as a replacement for fresh produce.

It took World War Two to persuade the British housewife that she could preserve summer fruits in bottles, and that it would taste every bit as good as the canned variety from the shop. Having once invested in bottling equipment, the habit stuck. Even today, many women possess the jars they bought then and merely replace the rubber rings or clips from time to time. At the same time various women's organisations have found it worth while to club together and invest in a canning machine, which members use in turn. In times of shortage, fruit is bottled in plain water to save sugar, but a sugar syrup is easy to make and gives both a better flavour and colour.

Bottling fruit

1. **Sugar syrup:** In general, soft and delicate fleshed fruits seem better suited by a heavy sugar syrup (such as raspberries, peaches) and harder fruit by a light sugar syrup (such as plums, gooseberries). But this is very much a matter of taste. It is usual to allow 6 oz. granulated sugar to each pint of water for a medium strength syrup; increase or decrease the amount of sugar by 2 oz. per pint to produce a heavy or light syrup respectively. Heat the sugar in water until dissolved, bring to the boil, and boil for 2 minutes. You can substitute either golden syrup or honey for the sugar, but this will colour the syrup and, in the case of honey, add a different flavour. It is possible to bottle fruit successfully in plain water, but it is much more trouble to sweeten the fruit afterwards, and takes at least as much sugar. The flavour never seems to be so rich and luscious as if the fruit has been bottled in syrup. On the other hand, too heavy a syrup makes the fruit rise in the bottle, and over-sweetens it.

2. **Brine:** A brine suitable for bottling vegetables is prepared by adding 1 oz. salt to each quart of water. Bring the salt and water to the boil, then boil for 2 minutes.

Preparing the jars for bottling

There are two types, one fastening with a screw band, and the other with a clip. In some cases the seal itself is made by a separate rubber ring, and these frequently need replacing. Rings which have lost their elasticity have perished. The latest type of jar has a lacquered metal disk to which a rubber ring is attached. This is very easy to use and a great time saver.

Rubber rings, tops and screw bands should be scalded, and jars rinsed out with boiling water, just before use. Do not prepare your equipment too soon, or it may become contaminated again before it is used. Discard any jars or glass tops with chipped rims, and any metal covers which are bent or have been stained by fruit acids. Do not wipe the insides of the jars dry.

You will notice some bottling jars have straight sides, and extra wide mouths. These are useful for large items, such as peaches and tomatoes, as they facilitate packing. Pack the jars as closely as possible without bruising the fruit, otherwise it will sink during sterilization and leave an unwanted space near the top.

Choosing and packing the fruit

Fruit should be ripe (not just under-ripe as for jam). It should be firm and unbruised. Bruised fruit can be used, provided the damaged parts are cut away, and should be packed in the centre of the jar so that it is not visible. Pack closely, using the handle of a wooden spoon to help you. Keep turning the jar, to make sure no awkward gaps have been left.

Bottling fruit for shows: Use a light syrup, as this allows the natural colour of the fruit to show through the glass. Pack very carefully, bearing in mind that the fruit should be evenly sized. This is often a winning point in judging bottled fruit. Sliced fruit should be arranged with the slices showing on the outside all facing the same way, layer by layer, in a definite pattern. Large stone fruit, such as peaches, should be halved and packed with the cut halves facing outwards, the hole left by the stone filled with a cracked kernel or a grape. Rhubarb should be graded to ensure that every stalk showing is the same thickness and trimmed to exactly the right length to fill the jar. The jar should be carefully polished and neatly labelled showing type of fruit and date of packing.

There are several methods of sterilizing bottled fruit, but these are generally the most successful.

Oven method

This is the easiest method, requiring the least equipment, but has the slight disadvantage that the fruit tends to shrink and discolour more than by any of the other methods given below.

Pack the fruit into prepared and warmed jars. Stand the jars on a wooden board, an asbestos mat or, if neither is available, a folded newspaper. Set the oven to gas mark 2 or 240°F. Cover the jars with a clean baking tray. Put any surplus fruit in a separate prepared jar which can be used to 'top up' the contents of jars which shrink down badly. Leave in the oven for $\frac{3}{4}$ hour–$1\frac{1}{2}$ hours.

Processing timetable

Raspberries and loganberries	45 minutes
Rhubarb, redcurrants, blackcurrants, gooseberries	50 minutes
Apples, plums, blackberries, cherries, damsons	1 hour
Whole or halved peaches and apricots, pears	$1\frac{1}{4}$ hours
Tomatoes	$1\frac{1}{2}$ hours

At the end of the cooking time, have ready a clean, dry wooden board, a pair of tongs or oven mitts for removing the jars from the oven, and the clean tops complete with clips, screw tops and rubber rings—whatever is needed for your particular jars. Lift out the jars one at a time. Have ready also a saucepan of boiling sugar syrup, or a kettle of boiling water. Fill each jar to overflowing. Put the rings, tops and screws on, tighten as much as possible. As the jars cool, tighten the screwbands every hour or so, until quite cold. Leave to stand for 24 hours.

Test for seal: Remove the screw band or clip and lift the jar by the lid. If the seal is perfect, there is no need to replace either

the clip or screw band, which can be used again. If replacing, grease lightly, and do not screw up too tightly.
Note: When required for use, lever off the lid by inserting the point of a knife between the rubber ring and the lid then gently levering upwards. If seal has failed, use up fruit at once.

Alternative oven method

This method avoids shrinkage and 'topping up' with more fruit.
1. Fill warmed jars with fruit. Fill to within 1 inch of the top with boiling syrup or water.
2. Put on the clean rubber rings and lids (not screwbands or clips).
3. Line a baking sheet with kitchen paper, and stand the jars about 2 inches apart on the sheet. Place in centre of oven.
4. Preheat the oven to 300°F. Process according to the timetable already given, increasing the time in each case by 10 minutes.
Note: Tomatoes, which are treated as a fruit for bottling purposes, should not be bottled in syrup. But they are improved if salt and sugar are added. To each pound of tomatoes, allow $\frac{1}{2}$ teaspoon salt and $\frac{1}{2}$ teaspoon sugar. Sprinkle into the jar as you pack it, and before adding any liquid. Use water or brine, as preferred.

Deep pan method

1. Pack the fruit into prepared and warmed jars. Fill to overflowing with COLD syrup or water. Tap and turn the jars to make sure the liquid has seeped through and all air bubbles have been expelled.
Note: Use brine for tomatoes.
2. Fix on the tops and clips or screw bands tightly; if using screw bands unscrew a quarter turn to allow for expansion.
3. Place a wooden slatted rack or trivet or thick piece of towelling or folded tea towel in a deep sterilizing pan, fish kettle, bread bin or deep saucepan. (The jars must not come in direct contact with the bottom of the pan.) Arrange the jars in the pan, not touching, and if necessary put pieces of cardboard between to prevent this. Cover the jars with cold water, and put the cover on the pan.
4. Place the pan on the lowest possible heat, then gradually bring the water to simmering point, 175°F. This should take approximately $1\frac{1}{2}$ hours. Maintain at this temperature for 10 minutes. Very large fruits, including whole pears, peaches, apples and tomatoes, should be maintained at 190°F. for 30 minutes.

5. Remove jars one at a time on to a wooden board using tongs. If you have none, scoop out sufficient water with small cup to enable you to lift out the jars with oven mitts. Tighten the screw bands immediately. Cool for 24 hours, tightening screw bands further if necessary. Clips should require no further attention. Use the same test for seal as for the oven method.

Note : All loose clips and screw bands should be washed, dried and greased before storing till the following year.

Problems with fruit

Small soft fruits, particularly raspberries and loganberries, should not be packed tightly, otherwise they form a solid block and are difficult to sterilize. It is best to use small jars for them, to make sure the fruit is sterilized right through to the centre without overcooking. The quantity of liquid needed depends on how closely the fruit can be packed without crushing. You will require about ½ pint of syrup or water to each 1 lb. jar. In a farmhouse garden, it is usual to pick the berries straight from the canes into the preserving jars. They can be cleaned by filling the jars with cold boiled water, and the impurities strained away by inverting the jar over the palm of your hand, over a sink.

Pears are also difficult fruit to bottle because they tend to discolour. They will keep a better colour if gently stewed in a light sugar syrup with sliced lemon, raisins and a pinch of powdered allspice. When tender, pack the fruit with the lemon and raisins into jars, bring the syrup to the boil again and pour in to overflowing. Cover and sterilize in the usual way.

Bottling fruit pulp

All imperfect parts of damaged fruit must be entirely removed, and over-ripe fruit should not be used, as it is likely to ferment.

1. Peel the fruit (or skin tomatoes) and cut into slices.
2. Stew the fruit, in just enough water to cover, to a pulp, with sugar to taste.
3. Scald the jars, tops and rubber bands.
4. Put the boiling pulp into the very hot jars.
5. Put on the rubber bands and tops, screw bands or clips. If using screw bands, unscrew a quarter turn to allow for expansion.
6. Stand jars in water slightly below boiling point, bring to the

boil, and maintain at this temperature for 5 minutes. Allow 8 minutes for tomatoes.

7. Lift out, continue the process and test as for fruit bottled by the deep pan method.

Tomato purée: Wipe the tomatoes, but do not skin. (They should be quite ripe; tomatoes which are not an even red colour are not suitable.) Heat in a saucepan with salt and water, allowing the same proportions as for brine, and sufficient water to come half way up the tomatoes in the pan. Cover the pan. When soft, rub through a hair or nylon sieve. Reheat until the purée starts bubbling, then fill quickly into warm preserving jars. Process as for fruit pulp.

Tomato juice: Wipe the tomatoes, skin by plunging into boiling water for 1 minute, then heat in a saucepan until soft. Rub through a hair or nylon sieve. Measure the quantity, then to each quart of pulp add $\frac{1}{2}$ pint water, 1 level teaspoon salt, 1 oz. sugar, and a pinch of white pepper. Reheat until it just comes to the boil, then fill quickly into warm preserving jars. Process as for fruit pulp.

Bottling vegetables

The process is perfectly simple, but it is now generally agreed that it can only be carried out safely if a pressure cooker is used. Vegetables, unlike fruit, do not contain enough acid to halt bacterial activity, and may be contaminated by certain bacteria which cause a dangerous form of food poisoning. Other processes suitable for fruit do not ensure that no living spores survive in vegetables.

When preparing vegetables for bottling, check that they are perfectly fresh and sound, and wash them thoroughly to remove any traces of earth. They must be blanched before bottling. Immerse the vegetables in boiling water for a few minutes, according to the blanching chart, then strain and rinse them in cold water until quite cold. This blanching process sets the colour, and makes vegetables easier to handle. It also shrinks them by about one third in volume. Drain well before packing.

Vegetable blanching timetable

Asparagus	Wash, trim, cut in even lengths	3 minutes
Broad Beans	Pod, using only young beans	5 minutes
Runner Beans	Wash, string and slice	5 minutes
French Beans	Top and tail	5 minutes

Carrots	Wash, scrape, slice or dice (leave young small carrots whole)	10 minutes
Celery	Wash, cut in even lengths	6 minutes
Corn	Strip from cob	3 minutes
Courgettes	Wash, top and tail, cut in even lengths	5 minutes
Peas	Wash, shell, using only small peas	3 minutes
New Potatoes	Wash, scrape carefully or peel thinly	5 minutes

Sterilizing by pressure cooker

1. Pack vegetables into clean, warm jars, leaving $\frac{1}{4}$ inch headspace.
2. Fill the jars with hot brine, just off the boil. Rotate the jars between the palms of the hands to eliminate air bubbles. Wipe tops of jars with a clean cloth. Adjust rubber rings and lids.
3. Adjust clips or screw bands. If using screw bands, screw down, then loosen by a quarter turn before placing in the pressure cooker.
4. Process the hot jars immediately. Put 1 pint hot water into the pressure cooker and add 1 tablespoon vinegar to prevent discolouration. Stand the jars on the inverted trivet. Do not allow jars to touch each other or the sides of the cooker. Put sheets of cardboard between the jars if necessary, and add an extra $\frac{1}{4}$ pint water to allow for absorption. Put on the cover, and place the cooker on a low heat. Leave control valve or vent open till steam flows freely. Then lower the heat and leave to steam for 5 minutes. This ensures that all air is exhausted from the cooker and jars.
5. Close the valve or vent and bring to **10 lb. pressure** on a low heat. Process according to the timetable given here, making sure the pressure does not drop below 10 lb. at any time.
6. Turn off the heat, or draw cooker aside and allow the pressure to reduce gradually at room temperature. Do not reduce pressure with cold water, as the sudden change in temperature may crack the jars.
7. Lift out the jars on to a dry wooden board. If screw bands are used, tighten each band at once. But do not attempt to adjust the rubber rings or lids in any way during the cooling.
8. The bottles will have lost much of the brine, which will have boiled away. This does not affect the keeping qualities of the vegetables.

9. The jars should be treated from this point onwards as for bottled fruit. When required for use, bring the vegetables slowly to the boil in the remains of the brine, or in fresh water.

Vegetable bottling timetable

Asparagus	40 minutes	Celery	45 minutes
Broad Beans	55 minutes	Corn	40 minutes
Runner Beans	35 minutes	Courgettes	35 minutes
French Beans	35 minutes	Peas	50 minutes
Carrots	45 minutes	New potatoes	50 minutes

Bottling fruit in brandy

Since the cost of fruit bottled in brandy is extremely high in the shops, it is worth the cost of the ingredients to do your own bottling at home. In many farmhouse kitchens, a few bottles are prepared when peaches are in season, and kept for Christmas. Other luxury fruits which are very good bottled in this way are pears, apricots, dessert cherries, raspberries and damsons.

The following method is useful when you are making up sugar syrup for bottling a batch of fruit:

1. Prepare the fruit in the usual way according to kind. Where the fruit has a rather tough skin (damsons, peaches, etc.,), prick with a darning needle four or five times, so that the brandy-flavoured syrup penetrates the fruit.

2. Make heavy syrup, allow to cool. To each measured pint of cold syrup add $\frac{1}{4}$ pint of brandy.

3. Cover the fruit with the syrup, and proceed to sterilize either by the oven method or deep pan method.

73

This alternative method is easier if you are not sterilizing other bottled fruit.

Remove hairs on 1 lb. peaches with damp cloth, but do not skin. Put 12 oz. sugar and ½ pint water into a saucepan and heat gently until sugar has dissolved, then boil for 8 minutes without stirring. Add the peaches, a few at a time, to the boiling syrup and simmer until tender, about 5 minutes. If the peaches are not covered by the syrup, turn during cooking. Remove the peaches with a draining spoon and pack into two 1 lb. jars. Cook the syrup for a little longer, then measure and add an equal quantity of brandy. Bring this syrup to the boil. Pour over the peaches and seal.

Note: Peaches bottled in brandy at the peak of their late summer season will be perfectly matured at Christmas.

Pressure pan method

Fruits, unlike vegetables, do not require to be blanched for sterilizing in a pressure cooker. Pack the fruit as for the deep pan method, then proceed as follows.

1. Fill the jars with BOILING syrup or water to within ½ inch of the top. Cover and fasten with screw bands or clips (unscrewing bands a quarter turn). Then proceed as in stages 4 and 5 for processing vegetables, with this exception: bring to **5 lb. pressure only** in the usual way. Continue processing as for vegetables.

Note: Most pressure cookers have an instruction leaflet which includes the use of the cooker for bottling. Follow the instructions given for your make of cooker if these are given.

Fruit bottling timetable—5 lb. pressure

Apples (quarters), Apricots, Cherries, Currants	1 minute
Damsons, Gooseberries, Plums, Rhubarb	3 minutes
Blackberries, Loganberries, Raspberries, Strawberries	3 minutes
Peaches, Greengages	4 minutes
Pears, Tomatoes (whole or halves)	5 minutes

Canning fruit and vegetables

It is essential to have a proper sealing machine. The fruit or vegetables and liquid (water, syrup or brine) are sealed in the can before processing. The canning machine is usually simple to operate, directions being supplied by the makers. The sealing is done in two stages. The lid is rolled over the flange of the can, then the lid and can pressed together to make an airtight seal.

Size of cans: Cans are available for use with most machines in 2 sizes, the 1 lb. size of 16 fl. oz. capacity and the A2½ size with 1½ pint capacity. There are three types of cans, each type being specially suitable for a particular purpose.

Plain cans: These are made of tinned steel plate, and may be used for light coloured fruits such as apples and pears, and all green and yellow fruit.

Fruit lacquered cans: These cans have a layer of golden coloured lacquer over the tin, and can be distinguished by the dimple in the centre of the base and lid. They are suitable for all fruits, but essential for red fruits such as blackcurrants, raspberries, rhubarb, and for tomatoes.

Vegetable lacquered cans: These have no dimple. The lacquer looks like the one used for fruit cans but will withstand the additional heat and pressure required for processing vegetables. They are often described as S.R. cans, being sulphur-resistant.

Rinse the cans in clean water before use, and if at all dirty, in boiling water. Invert to drain, and do not use a cloth to dry the inside. Discard any cans with scratches on the lacquered surface, and remove any dents in the flanges or rims.

Choosing fruit and vegetables for canning

All fruits and vegetables suitable for bottling are also suitable for canning, and the preparation is exactly the same. For the best results, try to get uniformity of colour, ripeness and size.

Packing fruit: Fill the cans to within ½ inch of the rim. Never over-fill as this squashes the contents. Rotate and tap the can to settle soft fruit. An A2½ can will take about 18 oz. fruit.

The same strength syrup can be used as for bottling, but it must be used BOILING. Remember that boiling a syrup for more than a minute or so will increase the strength, so do not leave it on the boil. Pour into the can to cover the fruit, leaving rather less than ½ inch space at the top. Put the lid in place at once, and do not on any account allow the contents to cool before sealing. Therefore, fill and seal only a few cans at a time. After sealing according to the instructions for your make of machine (which should be firmly screwed to a strong table), continue with the process, according to following instructions.

Processing cans of fruit: Immerse the cans in a water bath (a deep vessel with a false bottom or trivet, of any kind that has been mentioned as suitable for bottling) filled with boiling water. This will lower the temperature, so bring to the boil again. The following timetable is intended for use with A2½ cans, so if using smaller ones, reduce the boiling time by 5 minutes.

Canned fruit processing timetable

Fruit	Re-boiling Time	Processing Time
Apples, Apricots	5 minutes	15–17 minutes
Blackberries, Damsons	10 minutes	12–15 minutes
Gooseberries, Grapefruit	14 minutes	10–12 minutes
Greengages, Loganberries, Plums, Raspberries, Rhubarb, Strawberries	20 minutes	8–10 minutes
Black and Red Currants	5 minutes	18–20 minutes
Pears (dessert)	10 minutes	15–17 minutes
Pineapple, hard Plums	20 minutes	13–15 minutes
Tomatoes (quartered)	5 minutes	30–35 minutes
Tomatoes (whole)	10 minutes	40–45 minutes

Note: Tomatoes are canned in brine.

Processed cans should be taken out of the water bath at once and placed in cold running water until cooled to blood heat, to prevent continuation of the cooking process. Roll cans gently between your hands to test the temperature.

Packing vegetables: Fill the cans loosely to within ½ inch of the brim, but do not pack down too firmly. The same strength brine can be used as for bottling, but it must be used BOILING. Follow the directions given for bottling fruit from the point of filling the can, leaving rather less than ½ inch space at the top. The only difference is that canned vegetables must be sterilized under pressure, and require the use of a pressure cooker. The method is the same as that given for bottling vegetables, reducing the processing time for A2½ cans by 5 minutes, 1 lb. cans by 10 minutes. Remember to use the 10 lb. pressure control. Allow the pressure to fall at room temperature. Remove the cans and cool.

5

Salting, preserving and curing

Salting and smoking are among the oldest methods of preserving food. In the Middle Ages a large number of animals were killed off as winter approached and feeding stuffs became scarcer. The meat was then salted so that it would keep for winter use. Very often the cramped dwellings meant that the only available place for hanging the meat was over the fire and so, out of necessity, the second stage of curing (the smoking of the meat) took place.

The same necessity applied to fish, essential for fast days and for Lent, when meat could not be eaten. Most countries had their specialities. In Britain, we have our York, Suffolk and Bradenham hams, and other famous local cures for pork, a few of which are given here, besides smoked salmon and kippers.

A recipe for salting ham has been recorded as long ago as 200 B.C. In this country, since the days of Magna Carta, only the poorest homes have been without bacon, although smoking of course could only be carried out in the house when fires were lit, and it was often done in smoke chambers specially built outside.

Now most of the salting and smoking is done in factories, but the curing of pork is one of the oldest country crafts, and survives in many farmhouses, where open wood fires still burn in winter.

Salting is still very common, but the smoking process, which gives pork a far superior flavour and longer keeping properties, is less often possible. The old fireplace, with hooks in the inglenook for hams to hang in the smoke of the fire, is rarely used. Smoke chambers are not often seen. But sometimes a hogshead is inverted and used as a small smoke-house out in the yard. The smoke comes out through the bung hole and the hams are suspended from hooks driven in through the bottom. Sawdust, preferably oak, is used.

The season for killing pigs runs from November through to March, and a good sized animal provides a large family with fresh roast pork, pie meat, sausage meat, brawn, potted meat, pickled pork and green bacon for months, as well as with smoked ham and bacon. The joints most often cured are the ham and gammon, and the belly and flank. The ham is the whole hind leg, traditionally cut off round at the joint from the carcass. The gammon is the hind leg cut off square, and is usually divided into three: the hock, middle gammon and corner gammon. The ham is salted and then smoked if possible. The gammon cut, belly and flank might be pickled by the dry salt or brine method, and simply hung up to dry out thoroughly for a few weeks in a cool, airy larder. The temperature should be about 60°F., preferably with a current of air.

Equipment for home curing: This need not be elaborate but should include a boning knife, a carving knife, scales for weighing the meat, a large basin or tub for brine pickling and a curing trough or shelf for dry salting. One farmer's wife I know uses an old Victorian marble wash-stand for this purpose.

When using a wet pickle you will need some boards with weights to place on top of the meat, to prevent it from floating. Meat hooks and strong twine will be needed for drying the meat, and old pillow cases for storage.

Cleansing the meat before pickling: Immerse the joints in a strong brine. Make the brine by boiling together 4 gallons of water, 1 lb. saltpetre and 10 lb. salt. (Use rock salt, cooking salt or sea salt, but not the prepared iodised salt.) If the brine is salty enough, it will float an egg. Skim the brine, and when it is clear it is ready for use. Leave the joints in it for 24 hours. While the joint is in the brine, squeeze the large veins from the hock end to the fillet end. Remove the joint and drain with the fillet end upwards, but do not allow to become dry.

The curing process: This usually lasts up to three weeks, and may consist of immersing the joint in a wet pickle, turning it over each day, or in a dry pickle, turning it and rubbing it with the pickling mixture every day, or occasionally. Here is a Yorkshire housewife's description of a very simple method:

'The method for curing Yorkshire farmhouse hams and bacon is extremely simple, indeed the only ingredients needed are block salt and a little saltpetre. After shaping and removing the obvious blood vessels, blood and any bone splinters, the grated salt is rubbed in by hand and the saltpetre is used only on the bone and blood vessel points where possible. The meat is then left in a trough with the remaining salt for 3 weeks. After removing from the trough, the surplus salt is brushed off and the meat lightly washed and dried and hung up in a clean bacon bag, usually a pillow case, in a dry and airy room.' The joints are not cleansed by immersing in brine before curing.

The strong brine is, however, often diluted after being used for cleansing the bigger cuts, and used for pickling the head, trotters, tongue, etc. The length of time for pickling varies according to the thickness of the meat, to allow complete penetration.

Washing and Maturing: The joint is not always washed immediately after removing from the pickle. It may be left in the room where it was salted for a further few weeks to begin maturing, before being washed and hung up to dry. If the surface is encrusted with salt, soak it in water overnight first.

Drying: Hang the meat in a warm place, between 60 and 70°F., and if a thick crust of salt appears, remove it, as it attracts moisture. This is a longer, slower process than smoking, and it is essential that the pickle has penetrated thoroughly, or the meat near the bone may go rotten.

Smoking: Smoking over a fire introduces preservatives and flavouring substances into the meat. It is a quicker alternative to drying, but care must be taken that the temperature does not rise above about 85°F., as otherwise the fat will melt. Yet it is essential to remove sufficient moisture from the lean part of the meat. The ham should be turned from time to time, to smoke evenly.

Storing: If possible cured meat should be stored in the dark, at a temperature of about 60°F., but should never be allowed to drop to freezing point. Variations in temperature are to be avoided, and a dry atmosphere is desirable. In ideal conditions, hams may be stored hung up without any covering. Otherwise they can be surrounded by moisture-absorbing substances such as strong calico covered in a coating of kiln-dried salt. It is an old country custom to wrap the ham and store in a chest of sawdust.

79

Yorkshire cure

It is said that the original York hams were smoked with the oak sawdust which came from the building of York Minster.

14 LB. HAM	1¼ OZ. SALTPETRE
1½ LB. COARSE SALT	1 OZ. DEMERARA SUGAR

Lay the ham on a cold slab, rub with salt and leave for 1 day. The following day sprinkle the slab with salt and lay the ham on top. Rub well with salt and sprinkle all over with salt, saltpetre and sugar. Leave for 3–4 weeks. Take out of the salt, wash well in cold water, hang up in a smoke-house over burning oak sawdust, for about 3 weeks.

Devonshire cure

14 LB. HAM	3 GALLONS WATER
2 OZ. SALTPETRE	7 LB. SUGAR
2 OZ. PRUNELLA SALT	3 LB. BAY SALT
6 LB. COMMON SALT	

Pound together saltpetre, prunella salt and 1 lb. common salt. Rub this mixture well into the meat and lay in a large tub, turning frequently for 2 days. Put all remaining ingredients into a saucepan, bring to the boil and remove all the scum. Allow to boil for 15 minutes, then pour over the meat while still hot. Leave the ham in the pickle for 3 weeks, rubbing and turning it daily. Remove the ham from the pickle, leave to drain for 1 hour then cover with dry sawdust before smoking for about 3 weeks.
Note: Prunella salt is a special curing salt, obtainable from a chemist or herbalist. It speeds up the salting process and should only be used in small quantities.

Derbyshire cure

14 LB. HAM	1 PINT STOUT
2 LB. COARSE SALT	12 OZ. TREACLE
1 PINT BEER	¼ OZ. SALTPETRE

Rub the ham with 8 oz. of the salt and put into a tub. Put all the remaining ingredients in a pan and bring to the boil. Remove any scum and boil for about 5 minutes. Pour over the ham while still hot. Leave the ham in the pickle for 3 weeks, rubbing and turning it daily. Remove from the tub, dry thoroughly and hang in a calico or cotton bag in the kitchen for several weeks.

Leicestershire cure

14 LB. HAM	1 OZ. GROUND BLACK PEPPER
1 LB. BAY SALT	8 OZ. COARSE SALT
2 OZ. SALTPETRE	1½ LB. TREACLE

Rub ham all over with a mixture of bay salt, saltpetre, pepper and coarse salt. Leave for 4 days, rubbing and turning frequently then pour over the treacle. Leave for 4 weeks, turning and rubbing the ham thoroughly twice a week. At the end of this time, leave the ham to soak in cold water for 24 hours, then hang up to dry near a wood fire and smoke for 3 to 4 weeks.

To store hams: The hams should be put into calico bags or old pillow cases and hung in a cool dry place; alternatively they can be put into a box and covered with malt combs or broad bran. The Yorkshire way is to store them in a box packed with oak sawdust, and a large ham will not be at its peak of perfection in less than three months.

Baking a ham in a pastry crust: Wash the ham in cold running water and leave to soak for 24 hours, changing the water several times. Make a flour and water paste, allowing about 2 lb. flour and 1 pint water for a large ham. Mix to an elastic dough and roll out on a lightly floured board to a size large enough to enclose the whole joint.

Place the ham in the centre of the paste, damp the edges and bring together to completely enclose the joint. Put into a roasting tin and bake for 15 minutes in a moderately hot oven, 400°F., Gas Mark 6, then lower the heat to moderate and bake at 350°F., Gas Mark 4, for the remainder of the cooking time; allow 30 minutes to the pound.

When cooked, remove from the oven, break off the crust and remove the rind. The ham can then be finished in either of the ways suggested for a boiled ham.

Boiling a ham: First rinse the ham under cold running water, then leave to soak in fresh cold water for 24 hours, changing the water several times. Put into a large pan of cold water together with a good selection of vegetables and herbs, such as onions, carrots, celery, turnips, unpeeled apples, cloves, bay leaves; some people like to add a wisp of hay to give the ham a faint fragrant flavour. If liked, about 1 pint of cider to each gallon of water can be added, and/or 8 oz. sugar, and/or 1 lb. black treacle. The ham should then be very slowly brought to the boil and simmered gently for about 20 minutes to the lb. When the ham is cooked, leave it to become quite cold in the cooking water, then remove from the pan, drain and carefully remove the skin.

Ways of finishing a cooked ham: The quickest and easiest way to finish a ham after the skin has been removed is just to sprinkle it all over with freshly browned breadcrumbs and put a ham frill round the bone. However, a ham also looks most attractive if glazed with sugar and mustard, and if this is how you wish to finish the ham, reduce the cooking time by about 30 minutes. After the skin has been removed, carefully score the fat into diamonds and then spread with a mixture of brown sugar and mustard; allow 2 tablespoons dry mustard to 8 oz. sugar, or if preferred just spread with black treacle. Stick a clove into the centre of each diamond and bake the ham in a moderately hot oven, 400°F., Gas Mark 6, for about 30 minutes or until the glaze is golden brown. It is important during baking to cover all the lean parts of the ham with foil to prevent them becoming dry. When the glaze is golden, remove the ham from the oven and allow to cool. If the cloves appear to have become a little dry during cooking, replace them with fresh ones. Finally decorate the ham with a frill.

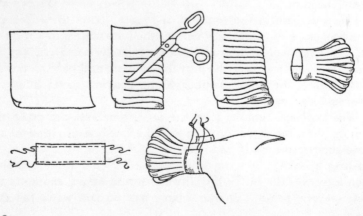

Making a ham frill: Small linen grip-bands used to be made from scraps of old sheets or table-linen. These were about 4 inches long and 2 inches wide, with a draw string running through each long hem. With these, a piece of white paper, preferably grease-proof, is needed, about 6 inches square. Fold in half, cut inwards in narrow parallel snips from the fold, stopping short 1 inch from the edge. Open out the sheet, reverse the fold to the other side, and wrap round the greasy end of the bone. Fix in place with the grip-band, draw up the strings and tie them in a bow for easy removal. The frill is thrown away and the grip-band laundered.

Salting beans: Beans are an ideal vegetable for salting as during their peak period even a few plants produce many more beans than can be eaten at one meal. It is not necessary to fill the jar all at once and it can be added to every day.

It is important to choose a suitable container; this should be either of glass or unglazed earthenware and should be wide enough at the top to enable you to put your hand inside to pack it firmly.

Choose fresh young beans and wash and string them. French beans should be left whole or, if very long, can just be broken in half; runner beans should be thinly sliced. For 3 lb. beans allow about 1 lb. salt. Use coarse cooking salt, as table salt causes the beans to go slimy. Pack the beans in layers with the salt, pressing down well between each layer and starting and finishing with a $\frac{1}{2}$ inch layer of salt. Cover the jar with waxed paper (not metal as the salt will corrode it) and leave for 2–3 days, after which time the beans will have shrunk in the jar and need topping up. Again the layers must be finished with a layer of salt. Cover firmly with waxed paper and leave in a cool, dark place.

To prepare the beans for serving, rinse thoroughly in cold water and then leave to soak in cold water for about 2 hours to remove the salt. Cook in boiling water (without salt) for about 20 minutes.

The great advantage of this form of preservation is that during the growing season you will usually gather more beans than are needed for daily cooking. The surplus can always be added to the bean jar. They will probably darken in colour during storage, but it helps to keep the jar in a dark place.

Salting nuts: Remove the shells of the nuts and throw away any that are withered or damaged in any way. Pack into a large glass or unglazed earthenware jar in layers with salt, starting and finishing with a ½ inch layer of salt. Cover with waxed paper and store in a cool place.

Salted nuts to serve with cocktails can easily be made at home. For 1 lb. dried shelled nuts, allow about 6 fluid ounces of olive oil. Heat the oil in a heavy frying pan, and gently fry the nuts in it until golden brown. Sprinkle in 1 rounded tablespoon of coarse cooking salt or celery salt and a little white pepper or cayenne pepper. Stir the nuts until they are evenly coated, then turn out into kitchen paper and spread out to dry. When completely cold store in airtight containers.

Another method of preserving nuts: This way enables you to preserve some of the nuts in salt and some in sugar. Shell the nuts (hazel nuts or filberts are particularly suitable) and blanch them in hot water for 1 minute. Rub on a clean cloth to remove the brown skins. Put a knob of butter into a thick saucepan, and fry the nuts to a pale brown. Drain on kitchen paper. Divide the nuts into two piles. Roll one lot in salt and the other in caster sugar while they are still hot. Allow to get cold. Store in airtight jars.

Dry pickle for beef

For about 7–10 lb. meat allow:

2 LB. COARSE SALT	½ TEASPOON GROUND BLACK
2 OZ. BROWN SUGAR	PEPPER
¾ OZ. SALTPETRE	

Rub the meat all over with half the salt and leave to drain for 24 hours. Pound remaining salt, the sugar, saltpetre and black pepper together in a mortar until a fine powder. Place meat in a large bowl or tub and rub the mixture well into the meat. Turn the meat and rub it every day for about 7–8 days.

Wet pickle for beef

For about 12–14 lb. meat allow:

2 OZ. WHITE PEPPERCORNS	½ OZ. BAY LEAVES
1 OZ. ROOT GINGER	2 LB. COARSE SALT
1 CLOVE GARLIC	6 OZ. SUGAR
¼ OZ. JUNIPER BERRIES	2 OZ. SALTPETRE
½ OZ. MINT	2½ GALLONS WATER

Tie the peppercorns, ginger, garlic, berries, mint and bay leaves in a muslin bag. Put salt, sugar, saltpetre and the water into a pan and gently heat to dissolve the sugar. Pour into the chosen container, add the muslin bag and stir round for a few minutes, bruising the bag gently with a wooden spoon. Add the pieces of meat and leave for 2–3 days, turning daily.

Note : Brisket and topside are most commonly pickled.

Pressed pickled beef

4 LB. PIECE BRISKET
8 OZ. COARSE SALT
¼ OZ. PEPPERCORNS

3 CLOVES
3 BLADES MACE
8 TABLESPOONS VINEGAR

Rub the meat all over with the salt, form into a roll and tie with string. Put into a bowl with cloves, peppercorns, mace, vinegar and sufficient water to just cover it. Leave for 24 hours, turning several times. Drain the meat and place in a large casserole with enough of the pickle to come half way up the joint. Discard cloves and mace, but add the peppercorns to the casserole. Cover and bake in a low oven, 325°F., or Gas Mark 3, for about 3 hours or until meat is tender. Cool the meat in the cooking liquor for about 1 hour, then drain. Put the meat between two boards, place a heavy weight on the top board so that the meat becomes pressed, and leave until quite cold.

Dry pickle for ox tongue

6 OZ. COARSE SALT
2 OZ. BAY SALT
½ OZ. SALTPETRE
8 OZ. BROWN SUGAR
1 TEASPOON GROUND MACE

½ TEASPOON GROUND CLOVES
½ TEASPOON GROUND CINNAMON
½ TEASPOON GROUND GINGER
½ TEASPOON FRESHLY GROUND
BLACK PEPPER

Mix all the ingredients well together, then put into the chosen container. Put the tongue into the mixture and rub it well in. Leave the tongue in this pickle for about 10 days, turning and rubbing it thoroughly every day.

To cook salted ox tongue: Thoroughly rinse the tongue in cold water and put into a large pan with fresh cold water, a bouquet garni, and a mixture of chopped root vegetables, such as onions, carrots and celery. Bring slowly to the boil, skimming frequently.

85

Cover tightly and simmer for about 4 hours or until quite tender. To serve hot, remove the skin and slice, or if wanted to serve cold, leave in the cooking liquor for about 1 hour, then remove the skin and any bones and roll tightly into a round cake tin. Taste the cooking liquor and provided it is not too salt, reduce it slightly by boiling rapidly and pour over the tongue. If the cooking liquor is too salt, use another good stock for this purpose. Put a plate on top of the tongue, weight it well and leave for at least 12 hours.

To cook salt beef or pork: Wash the joint thoroughly in cold water, and if liked, soak for about 2 hours in cold water to remove the salt. Put the joint into a saucepan and cover with fresh cold water. Bring slowly to the boil and simmer for 25 minutes to the lb. and 25 minutes over for beef, and 30 minutes to the lb. and 30 minutes over for pork.

Bath chaps

The 'chaps' are the cheeks of the pig, on which a piece of jaw bone and tongue are usually left. Bath chaps originated in the West country in the area round Bath, the local long-jawed pigs, fed on fruit, being especially suitable for curing in this way.

2 BATH CHAPS	$\frac{1}{2}$ OZ. SALTPETRE
2$\frac{1}{2}$ LB. COARSE SALT	8 OZ. SUGAR
1 LB. BAY SALT	3 QUARTS WATER

Rub the chaps all over with $\frac{1}{2}$ lb. of the coarse salt, and leave for 2 or 3 days, rubbing with salt and turning frequently. Put the remaining coarse salt, the bay salt, saltpetre, sugar and water into a pan and heat gently to dissolve the sugar. Pour into the chosen container and leave to cool. When cold, add the chaps and leave in the pickle for 2 weeks, turning daily. Drain well and smoke for two weeks.

Salt herrings: Herrings should be packed in wooden tubs with coarse rock salt and then left for several weeks before using. It is best to clean the herrings before salting, but it is not necessary to bone them. Put the cleaned herrings into a cask with the salt in layers, finishing with a layer of salt, until the cask is full, then firmly nail on the top and store in a cool dry place. To prepare the herrings for use, remove from the tub as many as are required, replacing the lid firmly. Wash the herrings thoroughly and bone if liked, then leave them to soak for 12 hours in cold water to remove excess salt.

Pickled herrings

12 HERRINGS	2–3 CHILLIS
3 OZ. COARSE SALT	2–3 BAY LEAVES
1½ PINTS WATER	2 PINTS SPICED VINEGAR
2 ONIONS	

Clean and bone the herrings and put into a brine made from the salt and water. Leave for 2 hours, then drain. Cut the onions into thin rings and roll up the herrings, skin side outwards, with a few onion rings inside each. Pack herrings into a wide-necked jar together with chillis and bay leaves, and pour over the spiced vinegar. Seal and leave for at least 5–6 days before using.

Smoked fish: Smoking is usually carried out commercially, following the time-old tradition of smoking over a fire, but these days it is usually a wood, rather than peat, fire. It is rather complicated and difficult to do at home, but if you are lucky enough to have a big catch you may find it worth while trying. The fish should first be cleaned and then, depending on the fish, they are either left whole (trout, buckling, smokies) or split (kippers, smoked haddock) or in the case of salmon they are usually boned. The fish are then put into a dry pickle for several days, before being hung up and smoked over a fire of peat or wood chips for 2–3 days.

Pickled bacon

8 LB. SALT	4 GALLONS WATER
12 OZ. BROWN SUGAR	2 SIDES PORK
4 OZ. SALTPETRE	

Put salt, sugar, saltpetre and water into a large pan, bring to the boil and boil for 20 minutes, skimming frequently. Pour into a large tub and leave to cool. When cold, put in the pork and leave for about 10 days, turning every day. Remove from the brine, dry thoroughly and hang up in a cool dry place.

Wet pickle for pork

1 GALLON WATER	6 OZ. BROWN SUGAR
1 LB. COARSE SALT	$\frac{3}{4}$ OZ. SALTPETRE

Put all the ingredients into a pan, bring to the boil and boil for 10 minutes, skimming frequently. Pour into the chosen container and allow to cool. When cold, put in the pork, and leave for about 3 days, turning frequently.
Note: Belly and head are the pork joints usually pickled.

To store apples and pears: Apples and pears which are required for storing through the winter should be picked from the trees very carefully so that the fruit is not damaged in any way. They should then be laid out on shelves, preferably slatted so that the air can circulate freely round them, in a cool dry place; an outhouse is ideal. The fruit must be spaced well apart so that if one does go bad it does not affect all the others surrounding it. During storage the fruit should be checked about twice a week to make quite sure that none is going bad and if you find any becoming over-ripe it is wise to use them as soon as possible, preserving them by bottling or freezing if necessary. There are certain types of these fruit, such as Russet apples and Conference pears, which do in fact only ripen on keeping and many of these will be ideal for Christmas when fruit in the shops tends to become expensive.

To store new potatoes: Using an old biscuit tin, sprinkle a layer of dry sand in the bottom, then put a layer of potatoes, about 1 inch apart. Cover with another layer of sand and continue these layers until the tin is full. Put the lid on tightly and seal with tape or elastoplast, then bury the potatoes in a sheltered place in the garden. The potatoes will keep until about Christmas time.

To store onions: This method was taught to me by a farmer's wife in Sussex when I was five years old, and I could soon make a very neat onion braid in a few minutes. Take three strands of raffia about 2 ft. long and tie tightly together at one end, trimming down to the knot. With the loose raffia ends towards you, place on top three dry onions with the withered stems towards you. Plait in one raffia strand with each stem twice, then lay three more onions on the plait, and weave in the new, longer stems with the

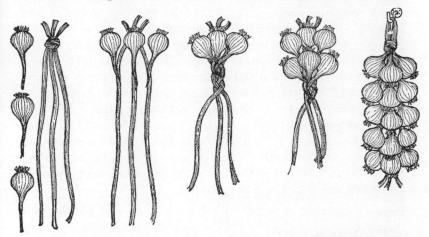

first three, and the raffia. Continue weaving in three more onions at a time. The raffia gives strength to the plait. When it is nearly all used up, tie one strand firmly round the last set of withered stems and tie all three strands together to make a loop. Use this loop to hang the onions in a dry place. If the onions are quite dry and a good keeping variety, they will last all winter and can be cut off as required, without removing the braid from the wall.

Preserving eggs

Butter method: A good old-fashioned way of preserving eggs is by sealing out the air with butter. The eggs should be as fresh as possible, clean and dry. Any dirt should just be wiped off; the eggs should not be washed as this destroys some of the protective film. Rub all over the egg with buttered paper, or if preferred brush with a little melted butter. Whichever way you choose to do it, it is most important that there is a thin layer of grease all over the egg so that the air is excluded. The eggs should then be stored in egg boxes, broad end uppermost. The egg boxes should not be airtight and cardboard boxes should have a few holes poked into the top to allow the air to circulate freely. Store in a cool place.

Eggs in waterglass: This is one of the most popular methods of preserving eggs. The waterglass solution should be made up following the maker's instructions and put into a stone crock or galvanized bucket. Eggs for preserving in this way should be at least 12 hours old and should be cleaned and dried. Do not wash them. Ideally the eggs should then be put into a basket and lowered into the solution which minimizes the risk of cracking. However, if this is not possible the eggs should be carefully put into the bucket or pail one at a time. Whichever method is used, eggs can be added to the pail all the time, provided they are kept covered with the waterglass solution. Care should, however, be taken not to make the layer of eggs too deep or the weight may cause the eggs at the bottom to crack. The bucket should be stored in a cool place and it is advisable to keep it tightly covered to reduce the loss of liquid from evaporation. Restore the level of the liquid with water if the loss is by evaporation or by more waterglass solution if any is spilt.

Preserving mint in sugar: Wash mint, drain well, pat dry on a clean tea towel and chop finely. Put a 1 inch layer in a jar and cover with an equal layer of granulated sugar. Continue these layers until the jar is full, finishing with a layer of sugar, then seal. To make mint sauce, mix with equal parts of boiling water and vinegar, as required.
Variation: Prepare the mint. Stir into a jar of clear honey until the honey has absorbed as much mint as possible. Use to make mint sauce in the same way as above.

Rosemary sugar: Clean and dry sprigs of rosemary. Pack loosely into a jar with a screw top, and fill the jar with caster sugar, shaking down and tapping the jar to make sure it fills in well round the sprigs. Leave a $\frac{1}{2}$ inch gap at the top and screw on the lid. Shake well, and leave for 24 hours. Shake again, and leave for a week, before using for milk puddings or other mild flavoured desserts. Lavender sugar can also be made in the same way and is delicious.

6

Drying vegetables,
herbs and fruit

Drying is perhaps, together with freezing, the most natural of all ways to preserve food. The early inhabitants of this country probably ate wild fruit and vegetables where they were picked, but as soon as people started carrying home the gathered produce, the problem arose of preserving some of it. It might have been left outside the cave on a rock in the sun, or hung up inside, out of the way but near the cooking fire. The methods we use today are not far different. The ancient methods, discovered perhaps by chance, rely on slow removal of all moisture. Even a slight hastening of the process leaves us with a wizened product which the most prolonged soaking and careful cooking cannot restore to its former luscious splendour.

The slow oven of the old country farmhouse range is ideal for drying, although if space is to spare, a great deal of produce can merely be hung from the rafters near the stove to dry gradually. The modern oven method is extremely simple, but there is an even older one, which involved keeping a stock of smooth, round wooden dowels which fitted across a roasting tin. Sliced apples were threaded on the dowels and suspended, row upon row, across the tin. During the winter, the young children not yet old enough to go to school used to play with these dowels, and use them to learn counting. On a wet winter's day, too cold and rainy for the children to play outside, I have seen a farmer's wife get out her stock of dowels, set them out in piles on the kitchen table, and give her two youngest, aged three and four, a brisk lesson in counting up to ten, then adding and subtracting small numbers. All done with dowels!

Oven drying and sun drying

Here are two methods of drying—either out of doors in the sun or in a warm oven. In this country with its unpredictable summers the sun method is perhaps something of a gamble and takes longer, but if you can manage to time your picking and drying to coincide with a heat wave so much the better. Both ways are given below.

Drying fruit in the oven

Most fruits will take from 4–6 hours to dry with an oven temperature between 110–150°F.

Apples (1): Choose firm, not over-ripe, apples. Wash, peel, core and slice into rings $\frac{1}{8}$–$\frac{1}{4}$ inch thick. Drop at once into cold water.

To prevent discolouring add 1 oz. of cooking salt to each gallon of water. When all apples are prepared, drain them well and pat dry with a cloth. Spread the rings with the edges slightly overlapping on baking trays or oven racks covered with cheese-cloth. Place the trays of apple rings in a cold oven and heat gently to about 110°F. Then open the oven door and allow the temperature to rise to 150°F. Test for readiness by squeezing—if no water comes out, the fruit is done. Be careful not to over-dry—it should be pliable but not crackle. As soon as it is ready, cool it as quickly as possible to prevent shrivelling.

Apples (2): After washing and drying the apples, cut into quarters. Remove the cores, then pare. (Save the parings and cores for jelly.) Dry the apples in a very slow oven until dry and leather-like.

Pears (1): Treat in the same way as **Apples (1)** but steam for 10 minutes after dipping in salted water.

Pears (2): Wash, dry and core and quarter the pears, which must not be too ripe. Dry in a very slow oven until like leather.

Quinces: Treat in the same way as in **Apples (1)** but steam for 10 minutes after dipping in salted water.

Plums: Gather the plums when ripe but not too soft. Do not peel. Wash and dry carefully. Halve and remove stones. Dry in a cool oven until quite hard.

Apricots: Peel, halve and remove stones. Dry until quite hard.
Currants: Top and tail. Dry until quite hard.
Damsons: As for Plums.
Grapes: Remove stalks but do not take out pips. Dry until hard.
Nectarines: As for Apricots.
Peaches: As for Apricots.

Drying fruit in the sun

Cut the fruit into slices approximately ½ inch thick. String the
slices on to thick thread or cotton, using a coarse needle. Each
string should be about one yard long. Hang the strings outside in
midsummer in strong, direct sunlight. Turn the strings occasionally, until the fruit is like leather. If the process takes longer than
a day, take the fruit indoors at night and leave it hanging in a
warm, dry place.

Storing dried fruits

Allow fruit to cool thoroughly after drying, and pack away the
following day. Fruit may be stored in paper or plastic bags with
the necks firmly fastened, or in muslin bags. These can then be
put into biscuit tins or similar containers with well fitting lids.

To cook dried fruits

Soak overnight in cold water, allowing 3 quarts water to 1 quart
fruit. Then cook in the usual way, sweetening if required.

Drying vegetables

The essential differences between drying fruit and vegetables is
that most vegetables must be blanched before the drying process.
For plunging the vegetables into boiling water you can use
either a wire basket or a muslin bag as a container. Except for
string beans (see below) it is not necessary to immerse the vegetables in cold water after blanching. Drain them, pat dry to remove
any surface moisture and then spread them in thin layers on
baking trays in the oven.

String beans: The delicate colour of the beans can be preserved
by blanching in boiling water to which salt and bicarbonate of
soda have been added (1¼ level teaspoons salt and 1 level teaspoon
bicarbonate of soda to 1 gallon water). Blanch for 5 minutes, then

immediately dip beans into cold water before drying as above. The beans will take from 3–4 hours to dry at an oven temperature of 110–145°F.

Carrots: Blanch for 6 minutes, then slice and dry for 2½–3 hours at oven temperature 110–150°F.

Parsnips: As for Carrots.

Celery: Blanch for 3 minutes, then slice and dry for 2–4 hours at oven temperature 110–140°F.

Peas: Blanch for 1–2 minutes then dry for 3–4 hours at oven temperature 110–140°F.

Pea pods: Delicious if picked young and sweet. Blanch for 3–4 minutes then dry for 3–4 hours at oven temperature 110–140°F.

Onions: Blanch for 3 minutes, then slice and dry for 2–4 hours at oven temperature 110–140°F.

Mushrooms: Thread the mushrooms on a string or thick cotton with a small piece of card or thick paper between each one. Hang them in the sun outside or in a warm oven to dry. Or take off the skin and stalks, thread through the centre and hang to dry upside down in the direct sunlight. This method will take several days.

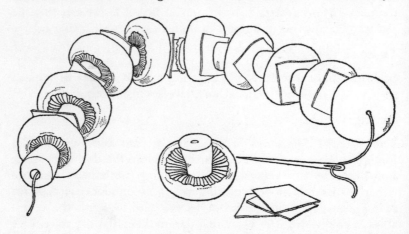

Mushroom powder: Place the mushrooms in a saucepan and cook over *very gentle* heat until the moisture has evaporated. Then place on baking trays in a warm oven until crisp, before crushing to a powder with a pestle or glass bottle. Store in an airtight jar. Soak the powder in a little cold water before using for soups, gravy or to flavour a casserole.

Storing dried vegetables

Vegetables must cool slowly for several hours or overnight before storing. Line large biscuit tins or similar containers with kitchen paper and store the vegetables in layers with a sheet of paper between each layer. Vegetables dried on strings can be left on the string and boxed as above.

To cook dried vegetables

The vegetables should be well washed and then soaked in tepid water for up to 24 hours. The longer the soaking, the shorter the cooking time. Cook in plenty of water (not the water used for soaking) and add a pinch of bicarbonate of soda. Bring *very slowly* to boiling point, allowing about 40 minutes for this. If the vegetables are cooked too fast at this stage they will be hard and unpalatable. After boiling point is reached, simmer gently for about $1\frac{1}{2}$–2 hours, then use as required for soups, stews, etc.

Storing in nets

Netting which was used to guard raspberries and strawberries from the avaricious birds in summer was often used in farmhouse kitchens for storage and drying purposes during the winter. It was twisted loosely round and round a stout stick which could be hung from hooks along the wall, or placed across two beams. The 'pockets' were filled with lemons, marrows, pumpkins and nuts.

Herbs

In the days when every manor house and cottage had its own herb garden, herbs had three main uses—in the cooking pot, the medicine chest, and the linen cupboard, where their refreshing fragrance scented clothes and sheets. Nowadays there is a renewed interest in growing herbs and town-dwellers often grow them in pots or window boxes.

Culinary herbs

Herbs to be used for cooking, such as thyme, parsley, mint, marjoram, sage and bay, should be gathered when at their most vigorous—just before they flower in most cases—on a warm, sunny day after any dew has evaporated. (Surplus moisture will cause mildew which would spoil the herbs and the result would be soft and flabby.) Tie the sprigs in small bunches and hang upside down, in a current of air and out of direct sunlight. After about 2–6 weeks the leaves will be quite dry and brittle. Thyme, marjoram and sage are known as 'sweet herbs', and can be stored mixed together by crushing the leaves finely with your fingers, mixing the resulting powders and putting into well-stoppered glass jars. Bay leaves are stripped from the stalk and used whole. In spite of the attractive appearance of rows of herbs on the kitchen shelf, it is better to keep these in your store cupboard as exposure to the light tends to spoil the colour.

Other herbs, such as coriander, dill, fennel and caraway, give seeds which ripen and brown on the plant—you need only collect them on a dry day when the sun has seen off the morning dew, and store them as above.

Bouquet garni

This is traditionally a small bundle or parcel of mixed herbs which is cooked with a stew or other dish and removed before serving. It usually consists of sprigs of thyme, marjoram, parsley and a bay leaf tied together or packaged in a little muslin bag. Other herbs may be added to these and can give interest and piquancy to flavour everyday dishes.

Aromatic herbs

Pot-pourri is a mixture of dried petals, herbs and spices which are kept in a bowl to bring the scents of summer into the house all through the winter. There are countless recipes for pot-pourri, some handed down for generations. Most of them centre round rose petals but you can experiment with whatever strongly scented flowers you have in the garden—the rules are not hard-and-fast.

Pot-pourri

On a hot, dry day gather a good quantity of roses—the old-fashioned cabbage ones, if possible—some lavender and carnations, some sprays of myrtle, rosemary, thyme and sweetbriar and geranium leaves, and a couple of sprigs of garden mint. Spread these out on sheets of newspaper to dry slowly in the sun. Two or three days should be enough but stir the petals about a bit from time to time to make sure the drying is even.

When the flowers are thoroughly dry, mix 1 lb. of kitchen salt with ½ lb. of bay salt, 1 oz. of powdered orris root, ½ teaspoon each of allspice and ground cloves, and a pinch of nutmeg. Add the shredded peel of 1 orange and 1 lemon. Put a layer of this mixture at the bottom of a large jar and top with a layer of flowers, then add the two mixtures alternately until the jar is full. Cover closely and leave for about a week, stirring occasionally with a fork. You can then pack the mixture into smaller jars or place in open bowls to scent the house.

Sweet herb pot-pourri

Gather equal quantities of scented geraniums, verbena, rosemary, bergamot, thyme, mint and bay. Tie them in bunches and dry for several weeks. When thoroughly dry, arrange them in layers, sprinkled with bay salt, ground cloves and cinnamon, lavender flowers and ground tangerine peel. This pot-pourri has a particularly delightful perfume and is ideal for putting into small bags to scent clothes and linen cupboards.

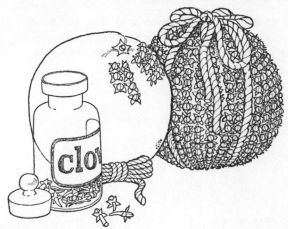

Pomanders

Originally carried to keep away the smells of medieval England from sensitive noses, these now make delightful presents to scent a room or wardrobe. Here are two which you may like to try.
Simple pomander: A tangerine is best for this, as it has a soft skin and a strong scent. Push cloves in all over the tangerine, leaving about one clove space between each. Press well in. Put to dry on a warm hearth or in the airing cupboard. Regularly squeeze the tangerine gently to press the cloves in, and go on drying

D

slowly until the fruit shrinks and the cloves touch one another. Continue drying until the tangerine is quite hard.

Flora's pomander: Take a small, thick-skinned orange and stick it all over with cloves as close together as possible. If you wish to hang up the pomander, arrange the cloves to leave a narrow space to encircle the orange twice and tie twine round it. (Replace this with silk ribbon or cord when the pomander is dry and hard.) Roll the orange in a powder made from equal parts of orris root and powdered cinnamon. Rub the powder well into the orange, wrap it in tissue paper and leave it for about a week before using to scent clothes, linen and so on.

Mint cushion

Dry bundles of mint, then use it to fill small cushions. These give a delightful fragrance to a room, and also help to keep flies away.

Old-fashioned lavender bags

Dry a good quantity of lavender and strip the flowers from their stalks; you need about $\frac{1}{2}$ lb. flowers. Mix thoroughly together with $\frac{1}{2}$ oz. of dried thyme and mint, $\frac{1}{4}$ oz. of ground cloves and 1 oz. of cooking salt. Put into small silk or cotton bags and sew up firmly.

Cheese-making
and cream dishes

When cheese-making started as a farmhouse industry in Britain, sheep were the animals most widely kept, so that it is not surprising that ewe's milk was the main source of the cheese made during the early and middle ages. In more recent times, cheese is made almost entirely from cow's milk. Similarly, old-established farm methods of producing cheese have become almost obsolete in so far as they involved the use of home-made rennet and of many types of simple equipment, ranging from brass and copper pans in which to curdle the milk and make cheese, to wooden moulds and stone presses in which to complete the process.

The development of the commercial dairy industry (which started in 1870 when a group of Derbyshire farmers, operating on a co-operative basis, established the first cheese factory) inevitably led to a decline of cheese manufacture on farms, but there still remains a small but flourishing farmhouse cheese industry in areas like Cheshire, Somerset and Dorset. Furthermore, there are still recipes for making both hard and soft cheese in a small way for the people who keep one or two cows of their own and who will, at times, have liberal supplies of milk which they want to put to profitable use.

Most counties have their special cheeses, as they have their special cures for ham. The Scottish wild garlic and herb cream cheese (now being made commercially) is a natural cousin of the

99

French Boursin. A rather more sophisticated version is the eighteenth-century English recipe given in the section on hard cheeses. Clotted cream is made from rich milk. The best cream is produced in the districts where special breeds of cows feed on rich pasturage, but in most districts there is a period where the milk produced is much richer in fat than at other times, and that is the moment to choose for experimenting.

Cheese-making

Hard cheeses: These are only a practical proposition for people who live on a farm or have access to milk in large quantities, as you need several gallons to make even one cheese of reasonable size. **You will need** a container to hold the milk, a drainer and cloth, a curd mill or tray for handling, cheese moulds or vats. Storage shelves in an airy room. Smaller articles include a thermometer, curd knife, small scales for weighing salt, larger scales for weighing curd. Muslin, cheese rennet, salt.

Clean and sterile utensils are essential; those that are easy to clean are obviously the best, and there are various items of everyday domestic equipment that can be adapted to a cheesemaking purpose. For instance: a zinc bath or enamel bowl as a container; a steamer top (the part with holes) lined with cloth as a drainer; if no cheese press is available, round cake tins with holes punched in do very well as moulds, and with a round piece of wood to fit inside the top, stones put on top of this provide the necessary weight for pressing.

Suitable milk: A first essential in the production of good cheese is good milk. Goodness for this purpose demands normal milk from healthy cows, cleanly produced and of average butterfats and solids-not-fat content. Milk which is very rich in fat, especially if the fat is present in the form of large globules, is not the most suitable for cheese-making, because of the excessive loss of fat which might take place during the process.

Other ingredients: Those most commonly used are rennet to coagulate the milk; salt to improve drainage, flavour and keeping quality; and a vegetable dye known as 'annatto' which is sometimes used to give the cheese—as some think—a richer and more appetizing appearance. It is now usual in large-scale cheesemaking to use what is known as a 'starter'. This is a culture of micro-organisms that provides acidity and flavour, but this first process can be dispensed with in the making of small amounts, and where speed is not as important as the personal touch.

Rennet suitable for cheese-making should not be confused with rennet essence, which is weaker and suitable only for the preparation of junket. It is essential that it should be in a purified form and as free as possible from micro-organisms. Reputable brands comply with these requirements. It should be stored under cool and dark conditions, and the use of stale rennet should be avoided.

Annatto suitable for cheese-making differs from that used for butter-making.

Salt for cheese-making should be of the highest degree of purity and a coarse-grained type is usually preferred, as, being less readily soluble than fine-grained salt, less loss occurs in whey drainage.

Treatment of curd: Initially, the curd for any variety of cheese is soft and tender, and the importance of gentle handling cannot be too strongly emphasized. If the curd is roughly handled during cutting and stirring, excessive loss of fat will inevitably take place, to the detriment of yield and quality in the cheese.

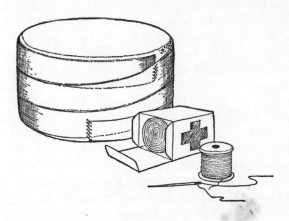

Ripening and storage: Most varieties of pressed cheese have a cloth bandage applied after pressing. The bandage serves to support and protect the cheese from damage during its subsequent handling. The most important factors in ripening are temperature and humidity. Where the temperature is above 60°F, ripening will be accelerated, but too high a temperature will lead to excessive evaporation of moisture and the production of a dry cheese. For general purposes, something between 55°F and 60°F will prove satisfactory, but from the standpoint of quality there are no disadvantages in storing the cheese at a lower temperature, apart from a slowing-up of ripening. While a high degree of humidity encourages moulds, a low humidity on the other hand leads to cracking of the rind and to excessive loss of weight. Varieties of pressed cheese are best ripened in a humidity about 85%. Shelving in the ripening and storage room must be kept dry and clean, and it is necessary to turn the cheese daily during the early stages of ripening to obviate softening of the ends.

Cheddar-type (1)

For a cheese of about 2½ lb.: Take 3 gallons of hand-skimmed milk from 3 consecutive milkings, i.e. 1 gallon from each. Warm it to 80°F. and then add ½ teaspoon plus 2 drops rennet per gallon, stirring it well into the milk. When set, cut the curd into large dice with a long-bladed knife. Warm it again slowly until the whey rises well. Gently bale off the whey from the curd; this can be done with a cup. Add 1 tablespoon coarse salt to curd, and with a milk skimmer or shallow wooden scoop put it into a steamer top (the part with holes in it) lined with muslin. On top of this fit a cake tin pierced with holes (a size to fit into the steamer), and set a heavy flat-iron in the centre of the cake tin or some other suitable weight wrapped in kitchen paper or clean cloth. Leave this overnight for the whey to drain away. Next morning replace muslin with a dry piece. Next day again, take the cheese out of the steamer, wrap it in dry muslin, replace it between two boards with the weight on top. Drying it with a rough cloth, turn it daily, until dry. If the cheese is inclined to crack, rub it with salt and then once more rub it with a cloth to dry. About the fourth day, bind the cheese tightly round with a strip of calico or bandage. This will keep it from becoming too flat under the weight. Leave bandage on till the cheese is matured.

Cheddar-type (2)

Heat milk (a mixture of evening and morning gathered is best) to 90°F. Add rennet—1 teaspoon to 3 gallons milk—diluted with 3 times its own amount of cold water. Deep stir for 2 minutes, then top stir until set, to keep the cream from rising. Leave about 50 minutes, then cut with a carving knife into small cubes (¼–½ inch).

Stir gently for 1 hour, gradually raising the temperature to 106°F. by dipping off some whey, heating this to 120°F., and putting it back on to the curd. Repeat this 3 or 4 times, until the whole is 106°F. Then gently pour off the whey, crumble up the curd and add 1 oz. salt to every 2 gallons milk. Put into a coarse cloth in the mould with 1 cwt. pressure. In the evening turn into a piece of muslin and put back into the mould and press again. The next day take the cheese out and grease it. Bandage and put in a room to ripen. Turn daily until ready for use. It can be eaten at 3–4 weeks old.

Banffshire 'picking' cheese

Heat the milk to 86°F. Add 1 teaspoon rennet to each 2 gallons of milk used. Set aside in a warm place until set into curd. Cut curd into cubes and drain off whey. Leave the curd overnight without salting it. Then break it up and set it outside where it can get really warm in the sun, taking it inside at night; repeat this process of heating for at least 4 days. By this time the curd should have quite a strong smell. If a strong cheese is required, the heating process may be continued for a week. Now add about 1 oz. salt to 3 lb. curd. Pack the salted curd into a mould and press for at least a week. Remove cheese from the mould, bandage it round, and put in an airy place to dry. Turn the cheese daily to ensure all-round drying. The important process in the making of this cheese is the exposure of the curds to heat. If it is not convenient to put curds out of doors, hang a pail of curd under a roof-light, where the heat of the sun is intensified by the glass.

Wensleydale

Heat the milk to a temperature of 90°F. Add $\frac{1}{2}$ tablespoon rennet to 9 gallons milk. Pour into curd trays. When the curd sets, break it up with a wire breaker, the proper tool, or a palette knife, and let it stand for 30 minutes. Take off the whey and hang the curds in a cheese-cloth to drip for 1 hour. Then crumble cheese into a mould with the hands (not too finely). Leave to stand for half a day. Then put the curd into a cheese-cloth and return to mould, weight and press. Next morning turn the cheese in the mould and press again. At night, take cheese from mould and put into brine. To make the brine bring enough water to cover the cheese or cheeses to the boil, and add salt until the liquid will float an egg. When it is cold put the cheese in. An 8 lb. cheese should be left in the brine for 3 days, and should be turned night and morning. Put a handful of salt on top of the cheese each time it is turned. When taken out of the brine, put on the storing shelf and turn every day until dry.

Shropshire sage

Add 3 gallons of morning milk to 2 gallons from the night before and warm it to 88°F. Stir well and add 1 teaspoon of rennet mixed with 4 teaspoons cold water, and stir for 3 minutes. Cover and leave to set. When solid cut into ½ inch strips with a long-bladed knife. Leave for 10 minutes, then break up carefully with the hands, stirring the whole mass carefully. Warm some of the whey and add to bring temperature up to 90°F.; keep on stirring till curd falls into smooth and firm pieces. Cover, leave 30 minutes, then push curds to side and drain off the whey. Cut curd into 6 inch cubes, leave 10 minutes; turn over and cut again, and leave another 10 minutes. Curd should now look dry. Break up fine and add salt to taste. Line a brawn tin with a cloth, pack curd in it, put a wooden cover on top and then a heavy weight on that. Turn next day and repeat if necessary. During ripening this cheese should be turned over every day and kept at least 8 weeks.

Sage can be added to the curd, both to colour and flavour. Either the whole of the cheese can be coloured or, as with Derby Sage, you can colour a centre layer of curd. To do this put a mixture of spinach leaves (to give colour) and sage leaves (enough to give flavour) through a mincing machine. Mix this with a little water and put into a muslin cloth and leave to drain. A third of the curd necessary to fill the tin is coloured by mixing it with the green liquid which has drained through the cloth. Thorough mixing is necessary and the surplus liquid is allowed to drain away. Half the uncoloured curd is placed in the tin and carefully pressed down. The coloured curd is then put in and pressed down before adding the remaining uncoloured curd to fill. The cheese is then put to press and subsequently treated in the usual way.

Caraway seed cheese

Heat 6 gallons of milk to blood heat, add 1 tablespoon rennet. When curd is set, break up with hands. Allow to settle for about 15 minutes, then pour off whey. Add 1 dessertspoon of salt to the curd; ¼ oz. caraway seeds; and 2 tablespoons fresh cream. Stir all together, and press into mould lined with muslin (or cheese-press lined with muslin). Weight and press if in mould or tin, leave for 3 days, turning each day, or adjusting sides of press as necessary, when cheese sinks. Keep for 2 months before eating.

Farmhouse gorgonzola

Warm 6 gallons of milk to blood heat; add 1 tablespoon rennet, and stir well. Cover the milk while setting. Leave for about 15 minutes, then break up curds with hands. Leave to settle, and then pour off whey. Mix 2 tablespoons dairy salt and 1 tablespoon oatmeal with the curd. Line a press with muslin or cheese-cloth, and press in the curd, altering position of press as cheese sinks. Leave in press for 3 days. Take out of muslin and place on a wooden board. Keep for 2 months to ripen, turning occasionally.

Here is an old English recipe from the Dales. Probably the cheese used was *Wensleydale*, or a similar type.

'Take a pound piece of fresh, crumbling white cheese. Grate it or crumble it very fine. Add to it 2 wineglasses of sherry wine, a small pat of fresh butter, and as much cream as wine. Add salt and fresh milled pepper to your taste, and herbs very finely chopped. A little of parsley, thyme, chives, sage, tarragon and marjoram. Put all in a pan when the heat is low, stir until smooth, and of a pleasing colour. Turn into small pots and keep in a cool larder.'

Cream cheeses: Usually there are two types of cream cheese, one obtained from double-thick cream, the other from thin cream thickened with rennet before draining, and there's a pleasant variety that can be made from buttermilk. A sweet cream cheese is obtained from cream that has been standing for 12 hours, but if wanting to make it more quickly a small quantity of 'starter' is put in as soon as new cream has cooled down to 70°F. This starter may be a culture generally used by cheese-makers, or a little clean soured milk.

The better the cream the better the cheese, yet many people think that almost any milk or cream will do for cheese-making. It must, at least, be perfectly fresh and sweet if the cheese is to be satisfactory. The old method of draining the cream by hanging up in a muslin bag or cheese-cloth and letting it remain some days is a mistake, as very often by the time the contents have stopped draining the cream will have acquired a bad flavour.

Double cream cheese

Take off the thickest cream into a clean can and stand this in a pail of cold water for several hours, then drain it through a fine longcloth spread over a wooden bowl or board. Use another board to press out superfluous moisture when drainage has taken place. Drainage and pressure should be gentle at first otherwise the pores of the cloth get filled with the cream. The cloth should be opened out once or twice and scraped during the first hour, after which the top board should be weighted. If the cream was thick and was well cooled before draining it should be ready to mould in 3–4 hours' time after weighting. Small moulds are used lined with strips of muslin or parchment paper for cheeses that are intended for sale, and a wooden palette knife is used for filling these; but for household use they would not be necessary as the cheese can be served on clean green leaves or in fancy dishes.

Single cream cheese

Very good cheeses from cream of a poorer quality can be made by adding 3 or 4 drops of rennet to a pint of cream containing perhaps only 25–30% of fat. The rennet should be added immediately after the cream has been cooled down to 70°F. It is skimmed up with a ladle, pressed for draining, and formed into shapes.

Milk cheese with a very small proportion of cream is made by mixing whole milk with some drained cream and a little rennet.

Buttermilk crowdie

Raise the temperature of the buttermilk to 140°F., holding it at this for 15 minutes and stirring continuously. Cool to 90°F. Settle for 20 minutes and then run off the whey. Ladle the remaining curd into a cheese-cloth on a draining rack and tie cloth, tightening as drainage takes place. This is usually complete in 6–8 hours. When ready it should cling together when pressed in the hand. Mix with a small quantity of good cream, and add salt at the rate of ¼ oz. to 1 lb. curd. This is ready for use immediately.

Cottage cheese

Place a jugful of sour milk in a warm place until the milk is quite thick, then salt should be added in the proportion of ½ small teaspoon to a pint. Stir well, and place in a muslin bag. Hang it up to drain overnight, press between 2 plates for 1 hour, then work up with fresh cream and make into a pat.

Clotted cream

Clotted cream is made by taking whole milk, warm from the cow, and straining it carefully into shallow pans. The pans should not be more than 7 inches deep and should be wide across the top. Set in a cool place, the pans should be left undisturbed for some 12 hours. After 12 hours or rather longer, the pans should be carried very carefully by 2 people and placed on the top of a stove or, better still, over a large boiling-pan containing boiling water, so that steam can play upon their contents. The cream should reach a temperature of 180°F. in about half an hour, after which the pans should be removed to cool off gradually. Heating should never be done too quickly or the cream will be greasy, and while heating over water is preferred it is quite often done over the ordinary kitchen range.

When the pans have cooled to their original temperature the cream can be taken off in the thick clotted condition that is usually seen, and it is better to do this in a sieve over which a piece of muslin has been laid as there may be some need to drain it; but if for immediate use, it can be skimmed into dishes straight away. One pound's weight of rich cream should be obtained from a gallon and a half of Jersey milk, but rather more is needed to produce the same from ordinary Shorthorns.

Curds

Curds and whey: New milk, from which no cream has been taken, makes the best curd and a little rennet, a very little, is used to produce the curd which should be taken up in a sieve and drained over a bowl. What comes out by draining is the whey, and this, when cold, is a most refreshing and wholesome drink. Sometimes curds and whey together are served in saucers with fresh cream and sugar on top. All methods of serving curds and cream make this an acceptable dessert, but in addition the curd is often pressed into a mould to exclude all whey and this solid curd is sold by weight for eating with cooked fruit.

Cheese-cakes from curds

Solid curd is often used for making a filling for pastry cases, and when so used is mixed with sugar, salt, spice, one or more beaten eggs, and possibly a few washed currants. A little milk added prevents it from setting too stiff after baking. The curd mixture poured into a lining of pastry in a pie-dish and baked until lightly browned makes a simple, wholesome pudding.

Skimmed milk

Milk from which all cream has been taken by a separator is often available at a cheaper price and is very useful for many cooking purposes, especially for making bread. For bread it should not be watered down, while for cakes and puddings it is good enough when a little butter is added to return the fat that has been taken away. For rice puddings butter may not be necessary, but it improves the flavour and adds to the nourishment.

Beestings

This is the rich milk a cow gives after she has freshly calved, and apart from its large cream content it also has the properties of eggs, e.g. a teacupful of beestings in a Yorkshire pudding is equal to 2 eggs, and it really does rise! Tarts can be made with it as you make custard tarts.

Beestings custard: Add two tablespoons sugar and a pinch of salt to 1 pint beestings milk in a pie dish. Stir well and sprinkle with a pinch of mixed spice. Cook it in a very slow oven, like an egg custard, until set.

Drinks made from milk and cream

Some very rich and satisfying drinks used to be made in farm-house and manor house kitchens; extravagant with the ingredients perhaps, by modern standards, but utterly delicious.

Rich syllabub

2 LARGE LEMONS	1 PINT DOUBLE CREAM
2 WINEGLASSES SHERRY	6 OZ. SUGAR
1 WINEGLASS BRANDY	

Grate the zest from the lemons and squeeze the juice. Stir the sugar into the juice until melted, add lemon zest, sherry and brandy. Add the cream, a little at a time, whipping steadily until very thick and foamy. Serve in small glasses.

Orange syllabub

2 SMALL ORANGES OR 1 LARGE
  ORANGE
1 TABLESPOON LEMON JUICE

3 OZ. CASTER SUGAR
½ PINT DOUBLE CREAM

Grate the rind from one of the oranges (or half the orange if using 1 large one) very finely. Mix into strained juice of other orange and the lemon juice. Add the sugar and stir until well dissolved. Add the cream and whisk until the mixture thickens. Serve in individual glasses or large glass bowl, chilled.

Hatted kit

Traditionally, the milk for this recipe was milked straight from the cow into the dish. Sometimes it is a mixture of the creamy milk and wine. In Scotland, the cow is milked into a dish containing warm buttermilk with sufficient rennet added to make it curdle. The whey is removed. The curd is seasoned with sugar and nutmeg, and blended with an equal quantity of whipped cream.

A Hampshire posset

Scald 1 pint of milk, and as it comes to the boil, add ¼ pint of white wine. Rub the zest off a lemon with a few lumps of sugar. Strain the curd from the drink, add the sugar lumps and a sprinkling of mixed spice, or equal quantities of powdered ginger and grated nutmeg.

Milk punch

6 EGGS
½ PINT MADEIRA OR SWEET
  SHERRY

6 OZ. CASTER SUGAR
1 PINT MILK
GRATED NUTMEG TO TASTE

Beat the eggs until very pale and foamy, add the sugar and wine, put in a double boiler over boiling water and continue beating until the mixture holds the trail of the whisk. Flavour the milk to taste with nutmeg, bring it to the boil, and pour it from a height into the egg mixture to make it very foamy. Serve at once.

8

Fruit cheeses, vinegars and syrups

Urban housewives consider themselves lucky to have any sort of larder, and often have to make do with a cupboard to store tins and dry goods. But the farmer's wife usually has a walk-in larder, and a large pantry as well. A well-stocked pantry is a source of pride. Visitors are often invited to take a look round the pantry, especially in autumn when it is brimming with row upon row of the new season's jams, fruit cheeses, curds, syrups and vinegars—not to speak of pickles, chutneys, sauces and battalions of bottled fruit. This is done in just the same spirit that a town housewife invites you to admire her new curtains or television set, and is expected to excite admiring sighs of envy and polite congratulations.

One Northamptonshire farmer's wife told me that a much respected rival in the household arts (a woman whose baking often beat hers at the local show) was due to pay her a visit in October. Not to be outdone, she drove over to her mother's farm and collected all the good soul's bottled jams and fruit on loan for the day. Her pantry shelves were fairly groaning under the weight of her own produce, plus that from another sizeable farm. 'Take a look in my pantry; it's been a fair year!' she invited. The rival looked, gulped, and was silent. It was a notable victory. I know of it, as I helped the victor to load and return all her mother's stores for the winter.

Some unusual fruit preserves

If you are confronted with a glut of fruit, and have bottled enough, and made sufficient jam for the family's needs, you will be interested in this chapter which includes a number of less everyday recipes. Some will probably be less familiar to many readers because the proportion of fruit required to produce the preserve is relatively high. They are not particularly economical to make unless you really have baskets of fruit at your disposal.

Fruit butters and cheeses are traditional country preserves and are usually made only when there is a real glut of fruit, since a large quantity of fruit gives only a comparatively small amount of the finished product. They are particularly useful in the case of fruits containing a lot of pips and stones, such as blackberries and damsons, as all the fruit is sieved before adding sugar. If you have a small child or someone on a gastric diet, this is the type of preserve to make.

Fruit pureés can be made from imperfect fruit if the bruised or diseased part has been cut away; it can then be pulped, bottled and stored. You can draw on this stock for pies and tarts and even for jam-making. Fruit that is too ripe for bottling or jam-making is excellent for making syrups. **Fruit syrups** can be used as a sauce to serve with steamed sponge puddings and similar sweets in the winter or with ice cream in summer. Some of them, such as raspberry, blackcurrant, or lemon, make a good drink when diluted with cold water or soda water, or with hot water in winter. **Fruit vinegars** are usually made with soft fruits and are used like a cordial; they used to be considered good for a sore throat. A fruit vinegar can also be used to replace a wine vinegar in salad dressings and so on.

Butters and cheeses

The fruits most commonly used are blackcurrants, damsons, quinces, apples and medlars. A mixture of blackberries and either apples or damsons makes a good cheese.

Pick the fruit over and wash it, and roughly chop larger fruits. Put it into a pan with just enough water to cover and simmer until really soft. Pass the fruit pulp through a nylon sieve, using a wooden spoon (metal can cause discolouration). Measure the pulp and allow the following amounts of sugar:

For butters: $\frac{1}{2}$–$\frac{3}{4}$ lb. sugar to 1 lb. of fruit pulp.

For cheeses: ¾–1 lb. sugar to 1 lb. of fruit pulp.

Return the pulp and sugar to the pan, stir until dissolved, then boil gently until the required consistency is reached (see below). Stir regularly, for as the preserve thickens it tends to stick to the bottom of the pan.

Butters should be cooked until they are thick like cream. The finishing point is determined by the consistency rather than by set or temperature, and the butter needs to be thick but semi-set so that it may be spread. Cheeses should be so thick that a spoon drawn across the bottom of the pan leaves a clean line.

Potting and serving

Butters: Pour into sterilized jam jars or small pots and cover as for jam, or use caps and rings as for bottling. Use or serve as you would jam, but do not store too long.

Cheeses: Brush the inside of some small jars or pots with olive oil; this enables the preserve to be turned out easily. Pour in the cheese. Cover as for jam and store for 3–4 months before using, as the flavour develops with maturity. Serve as an accompaniment to meat, poultry and game. Turn out whole from jar and slice at table.

Apple butter

3 LB. COOKING APPLES OR CRAB APPLES

SCANT 2 PINTS WATER OR WATER AND CIDER

½ LEVEL TEASPOON CINNAMON

½ LEVEL TEASPOON POWDERED CLOVES

¾ LB. SUGAR TO EACH 1 LB. PULP

Wash and chop the fruit, including the peel and cores. Add liquid and simmer gently until really soft and pulpy. Put through a fine sieve, and weigh the pulp. Return it to the pan with the spices and sugar. Stir until sugar dissolves, then boil gently until creamy in consistency, stirring regularly. Pot and cover in the usual way.

Grape butter

4 LB. GRAPES
WATER

½ LB. SUGAR TO EACH LB. PULP

Pick over fruit, remove stalks and wash. Put in a pan with about half the fruit's depth of water. Bring to the boil and simmer gently until fruit is soft and broken down, then press it through a fine sieve and weigh the pulp. Return pulp to pan with sugar, bring to the boil again and boil gently for about 1 hour, until creamy in consistency, stirring constantly to prevent burning. Pot and cover immediately in usual way.

Quince butter

4 LB. QUINCES, PEELED	WATER
1 LEVEL TEASPOON CITRIC OR TARTARIC ACID	½ LB. SUGAR FOR EACH LB. PULP

Chop fruit up roughly and put into pan, almost covered with water, and add the acid. Bring to boil and simmer gently until the fruit is soft and broken down. Press it through a sieve and weigh the pulp. Return to pan with the sugar. Dissolve the sugar, bring to the boil again and boil gently for about 1 hour, until creamy, stirring constantly. Pot and cover in usual way.

Blackberry cheese

2 LB. BLACKBERRIES	¼ PINT WATER
1 LB. COOKING APPLES (UNPEELED)	1 LB. SUGAR TO EACH LB. PULP

Wash the fruit and chop apples roughly. Simmer in water until soft. Rub through a fine sieve and weigh the pulp. Return to pan with the sugar. Dissolve sugar carefully, then bring to the boil and boil gently until a semi-solid consistency is reached. Pour into prepared jars.

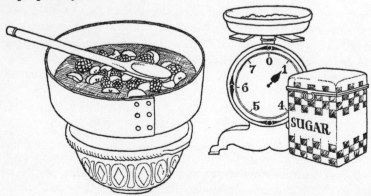

Medlar cheese

2 LB. MEDLARS	¾ LB. SUGAR TO EACH LB. PULP
2 LEMONS	I LEVEL TEASPOON MIXED
½ PINT WATER	SPICE

Wash medlars and cut each into four. Peel lemons thinly, squeeze out juice and cut up fine peel. Put medlars, juice and peel into a saucepan, add water and simmer gently until medlars are tender. Sieve and weigh the pulp. Add sugar and spice and return to pan. Stir, bring to the boil, and boil hard for 5 minutes. When it reaches semi-solid consistency, pot and cover in usual way.

Damson cheese

3 LB. DAMSONS	I LB. SUGAR TO EACH LB.
SCANT ½ PINT WATER	PULP

Wash the fruit, remove any stems, put fruit and water in a pan and simmer until really soft. Sieve and weigh pulp and return it to the pan with sugar. Stir until sugar dissolves, bring to the boil and boil gently until semi-solid, stirring constantly. Pot and cover in usual way.

Note: Many other fruit cheeses can be made as above.

Savoury fruit cheeses

Apple and mint cheese: Prepare apples according to the general directions for fruit cheeses, but just before the cheese is ready add 4 tablespoons chopped mint leaves. Cook for 5 minutes and pot as directed.

Apple and sage cheese: Prepare as above, but substitute chopped sage leaves for the mint.

Note: Both are excellent served with hot or cold lamb and pork.

Fruit curds

These should really be made in a double saucepan. They can be made in a saucepan with a thick base, if great care is taken to keep the heat low and to stir frequently. Fruit curds contain eggs and are therefore richer than butters or cheeses, but do not keep quite so long. If carefully potted they may keep as long as jam, but should be inspected for signs of mould from time to time and if possible, used up within 3 months.

Marrow curd

MARROW

LEMONS

SUGAR

BUTTER

EGGS

Peel the marrow and discard seeds. Put into a saucepan with
enough water to just cover the bottom of the pan and cook until
quite soft. Weigh the pulp and to each lb. of pulp add the grated
zest and juice of 2 lemons, 1 lb. sugar, 4 oz. butter and 2 eggs.
Put all these together in the top of a double saucepan or basin
over hot water and cook gently until thick and smooth. Pour
into hot sterilized jars and cover tightly.

Lemon curd

4 OZ. BUTTER

FINELY GRATED ZEST AND
  JUICE OF 2 LARGE LEMONS

8 OZ. CASTER SUGAR

2 LARGE EGGS

Put the butter and sugar into the top of a double boiler or basin
over boiling water. Stir until the butter has melted. Blend the
eggs with the grated zest, then strain over the juice. Add this to
the butter and sugar and cook over hot water until the mixture
thickens sufficiently to coat the back of a wooden spoon. Pour
into hot sterilized jars, cover and store for up to 3 months.
Variation : To make orange curd, replace the lemons by oranges,
but add the juice of $\frac{1}{2}$ a lemon.

Fruit syrups

Fruit that is too ripe for bottling or jam-making is excellent for making syrups; the best are blackcurrants, redcurrants, loganberries or strawberries, and any fairly small bottles can be used for storing them.

Seal bottles as follows:

1. With a cork, which must be cut off level with the top of the bottle and covered by a screw-cap.
2. With a screw-stopper.
3. With only a cork, but it must be tied on with wire or string to prevent it being blown off during sterilization.

Before use the bottle must be sterilized and any corks, etc., must be submerged under boiling water for 15 minutes.

Making syrups

1. Extract the juice. No water is needed except for blackcurrants ($\frac{1}{2}$ pint per lb.) and blackberries ($\frac{1}{2}$ pint per 6 lb.).

There are two methods of carrying this out:
a. Wash fruit and drain thoroughly. Place in a bowl over a pan of boiling water, break it up with a wooden spoon and leave until the juice flows freely (about 1 hour for 6 lb.), keeping the pan replenished with boiling water. This method ensures that the fruit is not over-cooked, which tends to destroy its colour and fresh flavour.
b. Wash fruit and drain thoroughly. Heat in a pan with the water (if necessary) and bring quickly to the boil, stirring constantly. Boil for 1 minute, crushing any whole fruit with a wooden spoon.
2. Remove from heat and strain overnight through a jelly bag.
3. Transfer pulp to a clean linen cloth, fold over ends and wring out as much juice as possible.
4. Measure extracted juice and add $\frac{3}{4}$ lb. sugar to every pint. Stir thoroughly over a gentle heat until sugar is dissolved.
5. Pour into sterilized bottles to within $1\frac{1}{2}$ inches of top, seal.
6. Place bottles in pan padded with folded teacloth or cardboard. Fill to the base of the corks or stoppers with cold water, then heat gradually to simmering point and maintain this temperature for 20 minutes.

7. Remove bottles. If using corks only, seal by brushing with melted candle wax when bottles are slightly cooled.
8. Store in a cool, dry place; the bottles may be wrapped in brown paper to preserve the colour of the syrup.

Elderberry syrup

I LB. ELDERBERRIES $\frac{1}{4}$ PINT WATER
I LB. SUGAR

Wash elderberries and put them into a double saucepan with sugar and water. Cook slowly without the lid, stirring occasionally, for 2 hours, or until liquid becomes syrupy. Cool a little, then strain into bottles, cork, sterilize as usual and seal.

Raspberry syrup

RASPBERRIES   SUGAR

Wash fruit and drain thoroughly. Put into large basin and stand over saucepan of boiling water, then heat slowly until juice begins to flow, mashing fruit with a wooden spoon occasionally. Remove from heat and strain through a jelly bag. Transfer pulp to a clean linen cloth, fold over ends and twist to extract as much juice as possible. Measure juice and add $\frac{3}{4}$ lb. sugar to every pint. Stir thoroughly over gentle heat to dissolve sugar. Bottle, cork, sterilize and seal.
Note : Redcurrant syrup—as above.

Rose hip syrup

Pick hips that are fresh, fully ripe and deep red. Crush, grate or mince them and put immediately into boiling water, 3 pints per 2 lb. hips. Bring back to boiling point. Remove from heat and leave to stand for 10–15 minutes. Strain through jelly bag and when it ceases to drip, return pulp to pan with another $1\frac{1}{2}$ pints boiling water. Re-boil and allow to stand as before, then strain. Mix both extracts, pour into a clean pan and reduce by boiling until juice measures $1\frac{1}{2}$ pints. Add 1 lb. sugar. Stir over gentle heat until sugar dissolves and boil for 5 minutes. Pour while hot into clean hot bottles and seal at once. Sterilize as for all other fruit syrups.

Fruit vinegars

Blackberries, blackcurrants and raspberries make particularly good fruit vinegars.

Usual method: Wash the fruit, place in a bowl, and break it up slightly with the back of a wooden spoon. To each lb. of fruit allow 1 pint malt or white wine vinegar. Cover with a cloth and leave to stand for 3-4 days, stirring occasionally. Strain through double muslin and add 1 lb. sugar to each pint. Boil for 10 minutes, cool, strain into sterilized bottles and cork.

Fermented raspberry vinegar

1 QUART RASPBERRIES	BOILING WATER
1 LB. SUGAR	BREWER'S YEAST
1 QUART WHITE MALT VINEGAR	

Pick over and hull the raspberries. Dissolve sugar in vinegar and pour mixture over fruit. Stir and mix well with wooden spoon. Strain after 2 days, pressing out all the liquid possible. Put the pulp into a bowl and cover with its own bulk of boiling water. Stir and let stand until cold. Squeeze as dry as possible through a linen cloth and mix with the vinegar liquid. Add the yeast, 2 level tablespoons to each gallon. Allow to ferment, and when fermentation stops, bottle. Store in a cool place for at least 2 months before using.

Fruit-flavoured brandy and gin

These are delicious extravagances that you might like to have in store for special occasions:

Apricot brandy

Cut up 12 fresh, ripe apricots into small pieces. Crush the kernels and add to the fruit in a screw-top jar. Pour in 1 pint of brandy and ½ lb. sugar; screw lid down tightly and leave for a month, shaking the jar frequently. Strain and bottle.

Pineapple liqueur

Slice a ripe pineapple very thinly, sprinkle with a little sugar and leave for 24 hours. Press out the juice, measure it and add an equal amount of brandy, and with sugar in proportion of 2 oz. to ½ pint brandy. Put in a screw-top jar with a few slices of fresh pineapple, screw lid down firmly. Leave for 3 weeks then strain and bottle.

Merlin's Magic: Add 1½ wineglasses of brandy to one bottle of dry mead. Serve as a liqueur.

Blackcurrant gin (cassis)

½ LB. BLACKCURRANTS	SUGAR
1 BOTTLE GIN	

Crush the blackcurrants and put with gin in screw-top jars. Secure lids and leave for about 2 months. Strain, and add 6 oz. sugar to each pint of liquid. Put in a jug, cover and leave for 2 days, stirring to dissolve sugar. Strain through fine muslin and bottle. Store for 6 months.

Sloe gin

1 LB. SLOES	4 OZ. SUGAR
FEW DROPS ALMOND ESSENCE	1½ PINTS GIN

Stalk and clean sloes. Prick all over with darning needle and put into screw-top jar with sugar and essence. Fill up with gin, screw down tightly and leave in a dark place for 3 months, shaking occasionally. At the end of this time, open the jar and strain through muslin until clear. Bottle and leave until required.

9

Bread, buns and scones

My own early memories of the glorious smell of bread baking are always mingled with the soothing, soporific sound of the dough being kneaded. I remember sitting curled up in a kitchen chair, watching a farmer's wife kneading, and rocking a cradle with her foot, in time to the rythmic slap and turn of the dough. It was I, and not the baby who fell asleep . . . Incidentally, she was the sort of woman who must have inspired the old country saying, 'Marry a girl who bakes and brews well, and she'll *bear* well.' It was true of her in every respect, for that baby was her seventh, and six of them boys!

The cradle, even then, was considered old-fashioned; has probably long since been banished to an outhouse, and may even now grace the window of a fashionable antique shop. But baking is still an integral part of farmhouse life.

Making your own bread

There are few things more satisfying than the smell, taste and look of home-made bread. Many people throughout the country still make their own bread, and home-made bread is being baked more and more by people who are finding the sliced and pre-packed loaf tasteless and dull. There are, however, many housewives who are put off by the idea that it is very time-consuming, complicated and difficult, but the making of bread can be adapted to fit in with your own time-table, and soon becomes an easy routine.

Important points when kneading bread: It is most important that the dough is well kneaded for about 10 minutes in order to obtain a good rise. When kneading, the dough should first be folded towards you and then pushed down and away with the palm of the hand. Give the dough a quarter turn and repeat this motion.

It is not essential for the dough to be left in a warm place to rise—in fact the dough will rise very satisfactorily in a refrigerator; the cold merely retards the growth of the yeast. Choose a rising time which will fit in with your day's plans. For a quick rise, leave for 45 minutes to 1 hour in a warm place; for a slower rise, leave at room temperature for about 2 hours. If you wish to leave the dough to rise overnight, it can be left in a cold larder for 12 hours, or for 24 hours in a refrigerator. If the dough is stored in the refrigerator it must, however, be brought back to room temperature before shaping. You may find it quite a good idea to make up a large batch of dough, bake some one day and store the rest in the refrigerator for 24 hours and then bake, thus ensuring fresh bread for several days.

If possible, always use *strong* plain flour for making bread as this will give a better rise and texture, but it is quite possible to make good bread using ordinary household flour.

In all the recipes in this chapter, dried yeast is used, as the majority of people find this much easier to obtain than fresh. If, however, you prefer to use fresh yeast, use double the quantity of yeast recommended. When making the yeast liquid, omit the sugar and merely blend the fresh yeast with the warm liquid.

Scones are one of the quickest and easiest things to make for tea time. They need not always be plain and can be varied in many different ways by adding dried fruit, cheese, spices, treacle or wholemeal flour or cooking on a griddle instead of baking.

White bread

3 LB. PLAIN FLOUR	1 TEASPOON SUGAR
1 OZ. SALT	1½ PINTS WARM WATER
3 TABLESPOONS OIL	1 TABLESPOON DRIED YEAST

Sieve together the flour and salt. Dissolve the sugar in the water and sprinkle the dried yeast on top. Leave for about 10 minutes or until frothy. Add yeast liquid to flour together with oil. Work to a firm dough which leaves the sides of the bowl clean. Turn out on to a lightly floured working surface and knead until the dough feels firm and elastic and no longer sticky. Put the dough into a large lightly oiled polythene bag, tie loosely and leave to rise until double its original size. When the dough has risen, turn out on to a lightly floured working surface and flatten to knock out all the air bubbles. Knead the dough until firm. Divide the mixture into 4 and grease 4 1 lb. loaf tins. Stretch each piece of dough into an oblong the same width as the tin and fold over in three. Put into the tins with the seam underneath, having first smoothed over the top. Put into oiled polythene bags and leave to rise until the dough comes to the top of the tins. Remove the polythene bags and bake in a very hot oven, 450°F., Gas Mark 8, for about 30–40 minutes. Turn out and cool on a wire rack. Makes 4 1 lb. loaves.

To make a cottage loaf: From each piece of dough, twist off one third. Shape the larger pieces into rounds, place on baking sheets. Damp and place the small pieces of dough on top, press the floured handle of a wooden spoon right down through the centre to the tin. Put to rise. Bake in the usual way.

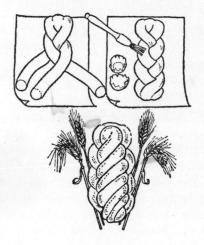

Harvest loaf

I LB. PLAIN FLOUR
2 TEASPOONS SALT
½ OZ. LARD
I TEASPOON SUGAR

SCANT ½ PINT WARM WATER
2 TEASPOONS DRIED YEAST
BEATEN EGG FOR GLAZING

Sieve together the flour and salt and rub in lard. Dissolve the sugar in the water and sprinkle the dried yeast on top. Leave for about 10 minutes or until frothy. Add to the flour and work the mixture to a firm dough which leaves the sides of the bowl clean. Turn on to a lightly floured working surface and knead well for about 10 minutes. Put into a lightly oiled polythene bag, tie loosely and leave to rise until double its original size. Turn dough on to a lightly floured surface and flatten to knock out all the air bubbles. Knead the dough until firm. Divide the dough into 4 pieces. Roll 3 pieces into strands about 20 inches long and join together at one end. Place on a greased baking sheet and plait loosely, tucking the ends underneath. Brush with the beaten egg. Divide the remaining piece of dough in half and roll into strands about 18 inches long. Join the strands together at one end and twist loosely. Lay this twist along the centre of the plait, tucking the ends underneath. Brush with beaten egg. Put into a lightly oiled polythene bag and leave to rise until double its original size. Bake in a very hot oven, 450°F., Gas Mark 8, for 30–40 minutes.

Malt loaf

1 LB. PLAIN FLOUR	3 TABLESPOONS MALT EXTRACT
1 TEASPOON SALT	2 TABLESPOONS BLACK TREACLE
1 TEASPOON SUGAR	1 OZ. BUTTER
GENEROUS ¼ PINT WARM WATER	CLEAR HONEY FOR GLAZING
1 TABLESPOON DRIED YEAST	

Sieve together the flour and salt. Dissolve the sugar in the water and sprinkle the dried yeast on top. Leave for about 10 minutes or until frothy. Warm together malt extract, treacle and butter. Allow to cool. Add malt and yeast liquids to the flour and work to a soft dough. If the mixture is too soft, add a little more flour. Turn on to a lightly floured working surface and knead well until the dough feels smooth and elastic and is no longer sticky. Divide the dough in half, flatten each piece and roll up as for a Swiss roll to fit two greased 1 lb. loaf tins. Put into lightly oiled polythene bags and leave to rise until they reach the top of the tins. Remove the bags and bake in a moderately hot oven, 400°F., Gas Mark 6, for 40–45 minutes. Turn out, brush the tops of the loaves with honey while still hot and allow to cool on a wire tray. Makes 2 1 lb. loaves.
Note: If liked, 4–6 oz. sultanas can be added to the flour.

Quick wheatmeal bread

8 OZ. PLAIN FLOUR	½ PINT WARM WATER
8 OZ. WHEATMEAL FLOUR	2 TEASPOONS DRIED YEAST
2 TEASPOONS SALT	SALT AND WATER SOLUTION
2 TEASPOONS SUGAR	FOR BRUSHING (OPTIONAL)
¼ OZ. LARD	CRACKED WHEAT (OPTIONAL)

Mix flours, salt and 1 teaspoon of the sugar together. Rub in the lard. Dissolve remaining sugar in the water and sprinkle the dried yeast on top. Leave for about 10 minutes or until frothy. Add the yeast liquid to the flour and mix to a soft dough. Turn out on to a lightly floured working surface and knead well. Divide dough in half and shape each piece into a ball. If liked, brush the top of each loaf with salt and water solution and sprinkle with cracked wheat. Put the loaves inside lightly oiled polythene bags and tie loosely. Leave to rise until double their original size. Remove the bags and bake in a very hot oven, 450°F., Gas Mark 8, for about 30–40 minutes. Cool on a wire rack. Makes 2 small loaves.

Flower pot loaves: When the dough has been kneaded, put into a well greased earthenware flower pot with a 5 inch top diameter. Put the flower pot inside a large oiled polythene bag, tie loosely and leave the dough to rise until double its original size. Remove the bag, brush the top with a little salt water and sprinkle with cracked wheat. Bake, standing the pot upright, in a very hot oven, 450°F., Gas Mark 8, for 30–40 minutes. Cool on a rack.
Note : When using a flower pot for baking for the first time, grease it well and bake empty in a hot oven once or twice to season it.

Wiltshire lardy cake

I LB. PLAIN FLOUR	½ PINT WARM WATER
2 TEASPOONS SALT	2 TEASPOONS DRIED YEAST
4½ OZ. LARD	OIL
I TEASPOON SUGAR	4 OZ. CASTER SUGAR

Sieve together the flour and salt and rub in ½ oz. of the lard. Dissolve the teaspoon of sugar in the water and sprinkle the dried yeast on top. Leave for about 10 minutes or until frothy. Add to flour and work the mixture to a firm dough which leaves the sides of the bowl clean. Turn on to a lightly floured working surface and knead well for about 10 minutes. Put into a lightly oiled polythene bag, tie loosely and leave to rise until double it original size. Turn dough on to a lightly floured working surface and roll out to a rectangle, about 15 inches × 6 inches. Dot one third of the lard over the top two thirds of the dough, fold uncovered third upwards and top third down over it. Seal the edges, give a half turn and repeat the process twice more so that all the lard is used. Roll out the dough to fit an 8 inch × 10 inch shallow baking tin, pressing it down well to fill the corners. Put into the lightly oiled polythene bag and leave to rise until double its original size. Remove the bag, brush with oil, sprinkle with sugar and make a criss-cross pattern all over the top using a sharp knife. Bake in a hot oven, 425°F., Gas Mark 7, for about 30 minutes or until golden. Turn out and cool on a wire rack.
Note : If liked, 4–6 oz. mixed dried fruit can be added after the lard has been rubbed into the flour.

Baps

I LB. PLAIN FLOUR	¼ PINT WARM MILK
I TEASPOON SALT	¼ PINT WARM WATER
2 OZ. LARD	2 TEASPOONS DRIED YEAST
I TEASPOON SUGAR	

Sieve together the flour and salt and rub in the lard until mixture resembles fine breadcrumbs. Dissolve the sugar in the water and milk and sprinkle the dried yeast on top. Leave for about 10 minutes or until frothy. Add the yeast liquid to the flour and work to a soft dough. Turn out on to a lightly floured working surface and knead for about 10 minutes until dough is smooth and elastic.

560g SWB flour.
        Salt
50g   Lard
2g   Yeast.
300ml warm water

handfull Raisens/sult.

add Sugar.

100g Lard
50g caster sugar.

gas 6½ 45mins.

Put into a lightly oiled polythene bag and tie loosely. Leave to rise until double its original size. Remove polythene bag, turn out on to a lightly floured working surface and flatten to knock out the air bubbles. Knead to a firm dough. Divide the dough into 10 equal pieces and form each into a round about ½ inch thick. Place on a floured baking sheet and dredge the top with flour. Put into an oiled polythene bag and leave to rise until double their original size. Remove polythene bag, bake in a moderately hot oven, 400°F., Gas Mark 6, for 15–20 minutes. Remove from the tray and cool on a wire rack. Makes 10.

Baking powder bread

2 LB. PLAIN FLOUR	½ TEASPOON SALT
2½ TABLESPOONS BAKING POWDER	2 OZ. BUTTER
	ABOUT 1¼ PINTS MILK

Sieve together the flour, salt and baking powder. Rub in the butter. Add enough milk to give a soft dough. Divide mixture into two and form into rounds about 1 inch thick and place on a greased baking tray. Bake in a hot oven 425°F., Gas Mark 7, for about 25 minutes or until bread sounds hollow when lightly tapped. Makes 2 1 lb. loaves. *Variation :* A similar type of bread without yeast can be made by substituting 1 tablespoon bicarbonate of soda for the baking powder, reducing butter to 1½ oz. and milk to 1 pint. Shape and bake as above or divide into four and bake on a floured griddle for about 12–15 minutes on each side. The bread sounds hollow when tapped.

Oaties

4 OZ. PLAIN FLOUR	3 OZ. BLACK TREACLE
2 TEASPOONS BAKING POWDER	4 OZ. MARGARINE OR BUTTER
½ TEASPOON SALT	COARSE OATMEAL FOR
4 OZ. ROLLED OATS	SPRINKLING
2 OZ. SUGAR	

Sieve together the flour, baking powder and salt. Add oats. Put sugar, treacle and margarine into a saucepan and heat gently until margarine has melted. Add to the dry ingredients and mix well. Press the mixture into a greased 7 inch sandwich tin and mark into 8 wedges. Sprinkle with coarse oatmeal. Bake in a moderate oven, 350°F., Gas Mark 4, for about 20 minutes. Makes 8.

Apple scone round

1 MEDIUM COOKING APPLE	2 OZ. BUTTER
8 OZ. PLAIN FLOUR	2 OZ. CASTER SUGAR
$\frac{1}{2}$ TEASPOON SALT	$\frac{1}{4}$ PINT MILK
3 TEASPOONS BAKING POWDER	1 OZ. DEMERARA SUGAR

Peel apple, remove core and grate coarsely. Sieve together flour, salt and baking powder. Rub in butter until mixture resembles fine breadcrumbs, then add caster sugar and apple. Mix to a soft, but not sticky, dough with a scant $\frac{1}{4}$ pint milk. Roll out the dough on a lightly floured surface to an 8 inch round. Place on a greased baking sheet, brush the top well with milk and sprinkle with the demerara sugar. Mark into 8 wedges. Bake in a moderately hot oven, 400°F., Gas Mark 6, for 20–25 minutes or until golden brown. Serve warm with butter.

Potato scones

1 LB. COOKED POTATOES	$\frac{1}{4}$ TEASPOON SALT
4 OZ. PLAIN FLOUR	1 OZ. BUTTER

Sieve the potatoes or put through a 'ricer'. Add sieved flour, salt and butter, mix well. Roll out thinly on a lightly floured working surface. Prick with a fork and cut into rounds or triangles. Lightly grease a griddle or thick frying pan and when hot cook the scones on each side until golden brown. Serve hot and buttered, with jam or honey. If liked, they can also be fried in bacon fat for breakfast. Makes 12–15.

Treacle scones

8 OZ. PLAIN FLOUR
PINCH SALT
4 TEASPOONS BAKING POWDER
2 OZ. BUTTER

1 OZ. SUGAR
4 TABLESPOONS MILK
2 TABLESPOONS BLACK TREACLE

Sieve together the flour, salt and baking powder. Rub in the butter and add the sugar. Blend the milk and treacle and lightly mix with dry ingredients. Cut into triangles. Cook on a heated griddle for about 7 minutes on each side. Makes 8.

Yorkshire scones

8 OZ. PLAIN FLOUR
$\frac{1}{4}$ TEASPOON BICARBONATE OF
  SODA
$\frac{1}{2}$ TEASPOON CREAM OF TARTAR
$\frac{1}{4}$ TEASPOON SALT
3 OZ. BUTTER

3 OZ. CASTER SUGAR
2 OZ. SULTANAS
$\frac{1}{2}$ OZ. CHOPPED MIXED CANDIED
  PEEL
1 EGG
MILK

Sieve together the flour, bicarbonate of soda, cream of tartar and salt. Rub in the butter until mixture resembles fine bread-crumbs, then add sugar, sultanas and peel. Beat egg and add to the mixture with enough milk to make a soft dough. Roll out to a round about $\frac{1}{2}$ inch thick on a floured working surface and mark into 8 segments. Put on to a greased and floured baking tray and bake in a moderately hot oven, 400°F., Gas Mark 6, for about 20 minutes or until golden brown. Makes 8.

Cheese scones

8 OZ. PLAIN FLOUR
$\frac{1}{2}$ TEASPOON SALT
$\frac{1}{2}$ TEASPOON DRY MUSTARD
PINCH CAYENNE PEPPER
2 TEASPOONS CREAM OF TARTAR

1 TEASPOON BICARBONATE OF
  SODA
$1\frac{1}{2}$ OZ. BUTTER
3 OZ. GRATED CHEDDAR CHEESE
$\frac{1}{4}$ PINT MILK

Sieve together the flour, salt, mustard, cayenne pepper, bicarbonate of soda and cream of tartar. Rub in the butter until mixture resembles fine breadcrumbs. Add cheese. Bind together with milk to form a soft dough. Turn on to a lightly floured working surface and roll out $\frac{1}{2}$ inch thick. Cut into rounds, using 2 inch

E

plain cutter, flouring the cutter each time. Put the scones on to a lightly floured baking tray and bake in a hot oven, 425°F., Gas Mark 7, for about 10 minutes or until well risen and golden brown. Serve with butter. Makes about 12 scones.

Yorkshire tea buns

2 LB. PLAIN FLOUR
$\frac{1}{2}$ TEASPOON SALT
2 OZ. LARD
2 OZ. CURRANTS
1 TEASPOON SUGAR

$\frac{1}{2}$ PINT WARM MILK
$\frac{1}{4}$ PINT WARM WATER
1 TABLESPOON DRIED YEAST
1 EGG

Sieve together flour and salt and rub in the lard. Add currants. Dissolve the sugar in the milk and water and sprinkle the dried yeast on top. Leave for about 10 minutes or until frothy. Add to the flour with the beaten egg and work to a firm dough which leaves the sides of the bowl clean. Turn on to a lightly floured working surface and knead well for about 10 minutes. Put into a lightly oiled polythene bag, tie loosely and leave to rise until double its original size. Turn dough on to a lightly floured surface and flatten to knock out all the air bubbles. Divide into 8–10 pieces and shape into round buns, about 1 inch thick. Place on greased baking sheets and put into lightly oiled polythene bags. Leave to rise until double their original size. Bake in hot oven, 425°F., Gas Mark 7, for about 25–30 minutes. Serve warm with butter. Makes about 8–10 buns.

Muffins

1 LB. PLAIN FLOUR
1 TEASPOON SALT
2 TEASPOONS SUGAR
SCANT $\frac{1}{2}$ PINT WARM MILK

2 TEASPOONS DRIED YEAST
1 EGG
1 OZ. MELTED BUTTER

Sieve together flour and salt. Dissolve the sugar in the milk and sprinkle the dried yeast on top. Leave for about 10 minutes or until frothy. Add to the flour with the beaten egg and melted butter and work to a soft dough. Turn on to a lightly floured working surface and knead well for about 10 minutes. Put into a lightly oiled polythene bag, tie loosely and leave to rise until double its original size. Turn dough on to a lightly floured working surface and flatten to knock out all the air bubbles. Roll out to a $\frac{1}{2}$ inch thickness and cut into rounds using a $3-3\frac{1}{2}$ inch pastry cutter. Place on a well floured board and dust the tops liberally with flour. Cover with oiled polythene and leave to rise until double their original size. Lightly grease a hot griddle or thick frying pan and cook the muffins a few at a time for about 8 minutes on each side when griddle is hot. Serve warm with butter. Makes about 6–8.

Crumpets

1 LB. PLAIN FLOUR	1 TEASPOON DRIED YEAST
1 TEASPOON SALT	$\frac{1}{4}$ TEASPOON BICARBONATE OF
1 TEASPOON SUGAR	SODA
1 PINT WARM MILK	1 TEASPOON WARM WATER

Sieve together the flour and salt. Dissolve the sugar in half the milk and sprinkle the yeast on top. Leave for about 10 minutes or until frothy. Add to the flour with the remaining milk and beat thoroughly for 5–10 minutes. Cover and leave to rise. Dissolve the bicarbonate of soda in the water, add to the risen mixture and leave to rise again. Lightly grease a hot griddle or thick frying pan and some $3\frac{1}{2}$–4 inch pastry cutters or plain rings. Place cutters or rings on griddle or frying pan and heat. Drop spoonsful of the mixture into the cutters and allow to cook until the top is set and full of holes and the underside a pale biscuit colour. Remove the rings, turn the crumpets over and dry out for a few minutes on the other side. Allow to cool. Serve the crumpets, toasted on both sides, with butter. Makes about 12.

Barm brack

¾ PINT WELL STRAINED COLD
    TEA
7 OZ. SOFT BROWN SUGAR

12 OZ. MIXED DRIED FRUIT
10 OZ. SELF-RAISING FLOUR
1 EGG

Put the tea, sugar and dried fruit into a bowl, cover and leave overnight. Sieve the flour and add the beaten egg and fruit mixture. Mix well. Turn into a greased and lined 8 inch round cake tin or 2 lb. loaf tin and bake in a moderate oven, 350°F., Gas Mark 4, for about 1¾ hours. Turn out and cool on a wire rack. Serve with butter.

Singin' hinney

12 OZ. PLAIN FLOUR
2 OZ. GROUND RICE
1 TEASPOON SALT
2 TEASPOONS BAKING POWDER

2 OZ. CASTER SUGAR
1 OZ. LARD
3 OZ. CURRANTS
½ PINT MILK

Sieve together flour, rice, salt, baking powder and caster sugar. Rub in lard and add currants. Mix to a soft dough with the milk. Roll out to a circle about ¼ inch thick and prick all over with a fork. Lightly grease a griddle or thick frying pan and when hot cook the cake for about 10 minutes on each side or until golden brown. Serve split in half while still warm with butter.

Yorkshire parkin

12 OZ. MEDIUM OATMEAL
4 OZ. PLAIN FLOUR
GRATED ZEST OF 1 LEMON
1 TEASPOON GROUND GINGER
4 OZ. BLACK TREACLE
4 OZ. GOLDEN SYRUP

2 OZ. SOFT BROWN SUGAR
4 OZ. MARGARINE OR LARD
4 TABLESPOONS MILK
½ TEASPOON BICARBONATE OF
    SODA

Mix oatmeal, flour, lemon zest and ginger. Heat treacle, syrup, sugar and margarine or lard until fat has melted. Add treacle mixture to the dry ingredients and mix thoroughly. Mix the soda with the milk and add. Beat well. Turn the mixture into a greased and lined 8 inch square cake tin and bake in a moderate oven, 350°F., Gas Mark 4, for 1–1¼ hours. Turn out and cool on a wire rack. Put into an airtight tin and store for a week before eating.

IO

Sweetmeats, crystallized and candied fruit

Gone are the days when children who lived on a farm only knew their tiny village shop, part post-office, part general store. One corner, and a shelf or two, would be devoted to sweets, often perilously crowded by adjacent supplies of tobacco, matches, stamps, bootlaces and bottles of cough mixture.

Visits to the village sweet shop were a delight. Toffee was chipped from the slab with a metal hammer, sticky sweets were sold unwrapped, and weighed up in a 'poke', that mysterious triangular bag in which one should never buy a pig. No wonder mother made up big supplies of sweets! They were cheaper, made of the best materials, and if not so gaudily coloured as the halfpenny and penny treats at the village shop, they tasted much better.

Nowadays farm children go to school by bus, and are subject to the same temptations as townies to spend their pocket money at the confectioner's shop. Yet there is something soulless about those pre-packed orderly rows of goodies, which seem to shrink in size and rise in price all too often.

The smell of sweets being made in a farmhouse kitchen was almost overpowering in its richness. The buttery smell of toffee rivalled the pungent peppermint smell of humbugs. Crystallized fruits appeared near Christmas, frosted orange and green and yellow. In spring and summer, whole primroses, violets and petals of bright pink roses were crystallized too, for cake decorations. As for the children themselves, they had their own specialities. They made treacle toffee, pulled candy, and the little ones, not to be trusted with boiling sugar syrup, made peppermint creams. At Easter they boiled and coloured eggs, writing the design on the egg with a crayon pencil, then wrapping it in onion skins for the boiling. This was always a job for the children, on every farm. And a box of mother's best butterscotch was often the first gift a boy made to his girl when he went courting.

Treacle toffee

10 OZ. SUGAR
2 TABLESPOONS WATER
2 TABLESPOONS BLACK TREACLE

2 OZ. BUTTER
1 DESSERTSPOON VINEGAR

Place all ingredients in a saucepan. Boil steadily for about 12 minutes, or until a small amount dropped in cold water forms a firm ball (300–310°F.). Pour into a shallow greased tin, about 8 inches square. When beginning to set, mark into squares with a knife which has been dipped in oil. Makes about 12 oz.

Granny's toffee

3 OZ. BUTTER
1 MEDIUM TIN SWEETENED
   CONDENSED MILK

1 TABLESPOON GOLDEN SYRUP
5 OZ. GRANULATED SUGAR

Use a pan with a thick bottom. Melt the butter over gentle heat. Add the sugar, condensed milk and golden syrup, stirring very carefully all the time. Allow it to cook gently for about 15 minutes, until the mixture turns a pale brown colour. Then turn it into a well buttered tin, allow to cool. Mark into squares. Makes 1 lb.

Burnt hazel-nut toffee

HAZEL NUTS (SEE RECIPE)
8 OZ. BROWN SUGAR
2 OZ. BUTTER

2 TABLESPOONS GOLDEN SURUP
1½ TABLESPOONS WATER
2 TEASPOONS VINEGAR

Blanch the hazel nuts, dry them and brown in the oven. Boil together the sugar, butter, golden syrup, water and vinegar—allow to boil for 12 minutes. Stir in as many nuts as the toffee will take and hold together. Pour into a buttered tin and allow to cool. Makes about 12 oz.

Toffee honeycomb

1 OZ. BUTTER	$\frac{1}{2}$ TEASPOON VINEGAR
6 OZ. SUGAR	1 TEASPOON BICARBONATE OF
2 TABLESPOONS GOLDEN SYRUP	SODA
2 TABLESPOONS WATER	

Put the butter, sugar, syrup and water into a large saucepan with a heavy base and stir over gentle heat until the sugar has dissolved. Boil steadily to 280°F., or until mixture forms a very firm ball when you drop a little into cold water. Remove from heat, stir in the vinegar and then the bicarbonate of soda. The mixture will rise considerably in the pan, giving the 'honeycomb' texture. Pour into an oiled tin. When cold, break into pieces. Makes 8 oz. *Note:* This toffee does not keep well, even when stored in a tin.

Butterscotch

1 LB. GRANULATED OR	3 TABLESPOONS WATER
DEMERARA SUGAR	3 OZ. BUTTER
$\frac{1}{4}$ PINT MILK	PINCH OF CREAM OF TARTAR

Put all the ingredients into a pan with a heavy base, heat slowly, stirring until the sugar is dissolved. Boil steadily to 280°F. or until mixture forms a brittle thread when you drop a little into cold water. Take off the heat while testing or it may burn. Pour into a buttered shallow tin, mark into squares before it sets. Break up when cold. Wrap the squares in waxed paper. Makes 1 lb.

Mint humbugs

1 LB. DEMERARA SUGAR
¼ PINT WATER
2 OZ. BUTTER

3 DROPS OIL OF PEPPERMINT
PINCH CREAM OF TARTAR

Put all the ingredients into a saucepan and boil to 280°F., or until the mixture forms a fine thread which can easily be snapped when you drop a little into cold water. Take off the heat, allow to cool for 1 minute, then pour on to an oiled slab. As soon as it is cool enough to handle, pull into long strips. Divide the mixture in half and pull half the strips until they become paler in colour. Twist the 2 strips together and cut into short lengths. Store in a tin. Makes 1 lb.

Treacle nut fudge

2 OZ. HAZEL NUTS
4 TABLESPOONS BLACK
    TREACLE

1 LB. SUGAR
6 TABLESPOONS MILK
2 OZ. BUTTER

Chop 1 oz. hazel nuts. Heat sugar, treacle and milk gently until sugar dissolves. Boil rapidly for about 5 minutes or until a little dropped into cold water forms a soft ball (240°F.). Remove from the heat and add butter and chopped nuts. Cool, stirring occasionally. When mixture is thick, pour into a well greased 8 inch square cake tin. When just set, cut into 1 inch squares and press a whole nut in the centre of each square. Makes about 1¼ lb.

Honey fudge

2 OZ. BUTTER
4 TABLESPOONS WATER
2 TABLESPOONS CLEAR HONEY

1 LB. GRANULATED SUGAR
8 TABLESPOONS SWEETENED
    CONDENSED MILK

Butter the inside of a large heavy saucepan. Add butter, water, honey, sugar and condensed milk. Stir over gentle heat until the sugar dissolves. Bring to the boil and then boil for exactly 10 minutes. Remove from the heat and beat well until the mixture begins to thicken. Pour into a lightly buttered tin and allow to cool. Cut into squares. Makes 1¼ lb.

Pulled candy

8 OZ. DEMERARA SUGAR
6 OZ. GOLDEN SYRUP
4 OZ. BUTTER

3 TABLESPOONS WARM WATER
1 LEVEL DESSERTSPOON GLUCOSE

Put all the ingredients together in a strong saucepan, stir over gentle heat until the sugar has dissolved. Boil to 265°F., or until a little of the mixture dropped into cold water forms a fairly hard ball. Pour the mixture into a buttered dish. When it is cold enough to handle, dust your hands with caster sugar and flour mixed, and form the candy into a ball, then 'tease' it (pull out long strands and knead them in again). When it becomes

pale in colour, pull into long sticks, twist them into walking-stick shapes, or cut into pieces with floured scissors and wrap in waxed paper. Makes 1 lb.

Variation: Old-fashioned cottage candy was made with two parts of treacle to one part of water and 'teased' in the same way. It was made into long sticks, these were dusted with icing sugar, then stood in a jam jar for the children to help themselves.

Lemon barley sugar

1 LB. LOAF SUGAR
¼ PINT WATER
1 DESSERTSPOON LEMON JUICE,
STRAINED

½ TEASPOON YELLOW FOOD
COLOURING
RIND OF 1 LEMON, FINELY
PARED

Heat all the ingredients gently in a saucepan, and stir until the sugar has quite dissolved. Bring to the boil and boil briskly, removing the lemon rind after a few moments. Continue boiling until the mixture cracks and is very brittle when a little is dropped into cold water. Remove from heat and allow to cool slightly. Oil a large shallow tin and roll the mixture into long thin strips. Twist and leave to set. Store in airtight containers. Makes 1 lb.

Nut-apple jellies

2 LB. SOUND COOKING APPLES 4 OZ. CHOPPED NUTS
½ PINT WATER ICING SUGAR

Slice the apples, leaving peel and core, and simmer with the water until cooked. Rub through a nylon sieve. Boil the fruit pulp until the liquid has reduced and it is quite thick. Measure the purée, and to each pint allow:

1 LB. GRANULATED SUGAR 1 DESSERTSPOON LEMON JUICE
1½ OZ. POWDERED GELATINE

Add the sugar to the apple purée and boil the mixture, stirring, until a teaspoonful dropped in cold water holds its shape. Mix together the gelatine and lemon juice, adding 1 tablespoon water, and stirring until the gelatine is dissolved. Add this to the apple mixture. Stir in the chopped nuts. Put into an oiled tin, allow to set. Cut into small shapes, roll in sieved icing sugar. Makes 1½ lb.

Quince crescents

5 LB. RIPE QUINCES (WEIGHED RIND AND JUICE OF 1 LEMON
   AFTER FRUIT IS PEELED AND PRESERVING SUGAR OR
   CORED) GRANULATED SUGAR
1 PINT WATER CASTER SUGAR FOR FINISHING

Cut the fruit into small pieces and cook in the water until quite tender. Rub through a fine sieve, then weigh the pulp and add an equal amount of preserving sugar. Return to the pan with the strained juice and grated rind of the lemon. Cook over a low heat, stirring continuously until very thick. Allow to cool slightly, then pour into shallow trays lined with greaseproof paper. Leave in a warm place, such as an airing cupboard or plate-warming oven of a kitchen range, for three days, until it is quite dry. Remove the greaseproof paper and cut into crescent shapes. Roll in caster sugar. Store in a tin in layers, separated by kitchen paper.

Peanut toffee apples

6 MEDIUM SIZED RIPE EATING APPLES
8 OZ. GRANULATED SUGAR
2 OZ. PEANUT BUTTER
6 SKEWERS OR STICKS

Wash and dry the apples. Do not peel. Insert sticks through apples firmly. Have ready a well buttered plate to stand the toffee apples on, and a bowl of cold water. Put the sugar and peanut butter into a heavy pan over a low heat, and stir until the sugar has dissolved. Bring to the boil, stirring all the time, and cook for a few minutes. Test by dropping a little of the mixture into a cup of cold water—it should make a slight crackling noise when it goes into the water. As soon as this happens, dip the apples into the bowl of cold water, then into the boiling toffee mixture, then once more into the cold water. Stand on the prepared buttered plate until set.

Honey balls (for children's coughs): Mix together in a small basin a knob of butter with half the quantity of honey and a few drops of lemon juice. Form into little balls, and let the child dissolve one in his mouth when the cough is troublesome or at night.

Coconut ice

1 LB. GRANULATED SUGAR
1 SMALL (6 OZ.) CAN EVAPORATED MILK
FEW DROPS COCHINEAL
12 OZ. DESICCATED COCONUT
OR 1 LB. FRESH COCONUT
ICING SUGAR

Dissolve the sugar in the evaporated milk over low heat. Remove the pan from the heat and add the desiccated coconut. (If using fresh coconut, it should be finely grated.) Leave to cool for a few minutes, then divide in two. Press the uncoloured portion into a loaf tin, lined with buttered greaseproof paper. Tint the other portion pink with cochineal, press on top. When quite cold and set, turn out and strip off the paper. Roll in icing sugar, and cut in slices. Makes 2 lb.

Sugar mice

2 LB. GRANULATED SUGAR	FEW DROPS COCHINEAL
¾ PINT WATER	I TEASPOON COCOA POWDER
3 OZ. GLUCOSE	I YARD CLEAN WHITE STRING

Put sugar and water into a pan with a heavy base, heat gently until sugar is dissolved. Add the glucose and boil to 240°F., or until mixture forms a soft ball when you drop a little into cold water. Allow to cool off the heat, without stirring, until it begins to thicken. Turn out on to a damp marble slab and when it is cool enough to handle work in the cochineal; keep turning into the centre with a palette knife until it becomes firm and opaque. Knead until the colour is even, then form into the shape of mice or press into mouse-shaped jelly moulds and turn out after a few minutes. Mould the ears separately and press into place. Work the cocoa powder into a small amount of fondant to colour brown and press on tiny balls for the eyes. Cut 3 inch lengths of string and press into the fondant for the tails. Makes 16 mice.

Fruit fondants

I LB. ICING SUGAR	CHOPPED NUTS, GLACÉ
2 EGG WHITES	CHERRIES, DATES,
I TABLESPOON STRAINED	CRYSTALLIZED FRUIT, ETC.,
LEMON JUICE	TO DECORATE
FEW DROPS OF ALMOND ESSENCE	

Sieve the icing sugar, and mix in a basin with the egg whites, lemon juice and almond essence. The mixture will form a stiff dough. Beat until the mixture is really smooth. Roll out and form into squares, crescents, rounds, ovals etc. Press a piece of chopped fruit or nut firmly into the top of each. Makes 1¼ lb.

Peppermint creams

1 LB. ICING SUGAR
1 EGG WHITE
½ GILL DOUBLE CREAM

FEW DROPS PEPPERMINT
ESSENCE TO TASTE

Sift the icing sugar and mix with the egg white and cream. Blend mixture thoroughly and add peppermint essence to taste. Roll out on a board well dusted with icing sugar, and cut out into small circles or half moons. Move creams carefully on to a wire rack and allow to dry out overnight. Makes 1¼ lb.

Marzipan potatoes

8 OZ. GROUND ALMONDS
4 OZ. CASTER SUGAR
4 OZ. ICING SUGAR

FEW DROPS ALMOND ESSENCE
2 EGG YOLKS
COCOA POWDER

Mix all the ingredients except cocoa together, and form into small balls. Prick with a knitting needle to simulate the eyes of potatoes, then roll in cocoa powder. Allow to dry on a clean baking sheet. Makes 1 lb.

Marzipan treats

6 OZ. GRANULATED SUGAR
¼ PINT WATER
4 OZ. BUTTER
2 OZ. GROUND ALMONDS
FEW DROPS VANILLA
  ESSENCE

2 OZ. CHOPPED GLACÉ
  CHERRIES
2 OZ. CHOPPED WALNUTS
4 OZ. FINE SEMOLINA
FEW DROPS ALMOND
  ESSENCE

Boil the sugar and water together to a thick syrup, and remove from the heat before the colour deepens. Melt the butter, stir in the semolina and brown lightly. Add ground almonds and almond and vanilla essence. Add this to the syrup, stirring continuously over a low heat and until it thickens. Cook for a further 2 minutes. Allow to cool, then roll out on a board dusted with icing sugar.

Scatter the chopped cherries and walnuts over and roll into a swiss roll shape. Wrap in greaseproof paper and leave in refrigerator overnight. Slice into ½ inch widths. Makes about 1 lb.

Candied peel

4 ORANGES   ½ OZ. BICARBONATE OF SODA
4 LEMONS   1½ LB. GRANULATED SUGAR

Wash the fruit and slice in half, cutting the lemons lengthwise, the oranges crosswise. Remove all pulp. Dissolve the bicarbonate of soda in ¼ pint of hot water and pour over each piece of peel. Add sufficient boiling water to cover peel completely. Allow to stand for 20 minutes. Rinse very well. Cover peel with cold water and bring to boil, then simmer until tender. Make a sugar syrup from 1 lb. sugar and ¾ pint water. Pour this over the peel and stand for 2 days. Strain off the syrup and mix into it a further ½ lb. sugar. Bring this slowly to the boil and simmer the peel in it until it looks clear. Lift the peel out and dry it slowly on trays in a cool oven. Reduce the syrup by boiling for ½ hour. Dip the peel into the syrup and dry again in the oven. Boil up the remaining syrup until it is cloudy and thick. Pour a very little into each candied cup. Allow to dry, and then store in airtight containers. Makes 16 pieces.

Preserved angelica

ANGELICA   GRANULATED SUGAR

Choose young stems of angelica for preserving. Cut them into matching lengths and boil until tender. Remove from the water and strip off the outer skin, then return to the pan and simmer very slowly until they are green. Dry well, then weigh. Allow 1 lb. granulated sugar to each lb. of angelica. Place the stems in a shallow dish and sprinkle the sugar over them. Leave them for 2 days and then boil the sugar and stems well together. When thoroughly boiled, remove the angelica and add 2 oz. of granulated sugar to the existing syrup. Boil this, then add the angelica and boil for a further 5 minutes. Drain the angelica and spread it on a tray in a cool oven to dry.

Marrons glacé

I LB. LARGE CHESTNUTS   ¼ PINT WATER
I LB. GRANULATED SUGAR   ½ TEASPOON VANILLA ESSENCE

Gently slit the skins of the chestnuts with a sharp knife, but be careful not to cut into the nuts. Boil the nuts for 20 minutes, then skin them while still warm. Make a syrup from the sugar and water, stirring to dissolve the sugar and boiling them together. Add the vanilla essence and chestnuts. Boil briskly for 10 minutes, then take the nuts out and drain them on a wire rack. Leave for 24 hours, then re-boil the syrup, put the nuts back and simmer until they are thickly coated. Drain as before, and allow to dry before putting into airtight containers. Makes 1½ lb.

Crystallized flowers

These are most attractive either by themselves or when used as decorations for other sweets and puddings. Flowers should be picked on a dry sunny day when the dew has dried from them—choose violets, primroses, roses and the blossom of plums, apples and cherries and pears. Not all flowers are edible so do not be tempted to experiment unless you are certain the flower is not poisonous.

WHOLE FLOWERS OR FLOWER   TRIPLE STRENGTH ROSEWATER
    PETALS   CASTER SUGAR
I OZ. GUM ARABIC

Put the gum arabic into a small bowl and cover with the rosewater. Leave for 24 hours. When the gum arabic has melted, carefully paint it over each flower petal, using a fine paint brush. Make sure that the petals are completely coated on both sides. Sprinkle all over with caster sugar, and store carefully laid on layers of greaseproof paper.

Crystallized grapes and oranges

ORANGES

SUGAR SYRUP (SEE RECIPE)

GRAPES (FRUIT SHOULD BE

SEEDLESS IF POSSIBLE)

Divide oranges into sections, removing peel and pith but being careful not to break the inside skin. Take grapes from the bunch leaving a short stem attached to each. Weigh the fruit and allow ½ pint syrup to each lb. of fruit. (The syrup should be made from ½ pint water boiled up with 6 oz. granulated sugar.) Put the fruit into a shallow dish and pour the syrup over while still warm. Cover and leave for 24 hours. Pour off the syrup and re-boil, adding another 2 oz. sugar. Pour over fruit again and leave for a further 24 hours. Repeat the process 3 more times, adding 2 oz. extra sugar to the syrup before each boiling. Drain the syrup again and return it to the pan, adding 3 oz. more sugar, and boil. When boiling add the fruit and keep boiling for 3 minutes. Pour fruit and syrup back into dish and leave for 24 hours. Repeat the boiling process with another 3 oz. sugar, then drain the syrup from the fruit thoroughly, using a wire tray. To give a crisp finish to the fruit, put the tray into a cool oven (200°F.—Gas Mark ¼) and leave the oven door slightly ajar. Take out when crisp.

Crystallized tomatoes

LARGE TOMATOES

¾ LB. SUGAR

1 PINT WATER

EXTRA SUGAR FOR FINISHING

Wash the tomatoes and cut four small slits near the bottom of each without breaking them. Squeeze out as many of the seeds as possible. Make a thick syrup by boiling the sugar with the water, stirring until the sugar has dissolved. When the syrup has thickened, add the tomatoes carefully and boil for about 3 minutes. Remove from the syrup, roll tomatoes in sugar and put on an oiled dish in the sun to dry.

II

Potted meats,
moulds and pies

Many of the most delicious farmhouse delicacies are made from parts of the animal a town housewife never sees in her butcher's shop. In fact she could not be blamed for imagining that her meat came from a new breed of beast, without head, hoof or trotters! When a pig, for instance, is killed on a farm, every part is used in some way, and it is quite an everyday matter. Most farmers' wives are capable of tackling a sheep's head, or even an ox head.

I was rather disturbed the first time I saw a sheep's head being salted ready for making brawn. Fortunately I did not associate the gruesome object on the kitchen table with my favourite pet, an orphan lamb the farmer's wife was raising by hand, although it was probably the head of a close relative! I came twice daily to that farm for the privilege of giving my pet lamb his bottle, and it took some courage, for there was a particularly fearsome watch dog in the yard, and I trembled as I scurried past, clutching the empty milk can, which was my excuse for coming, like a talisman. I used to try and cuddle my pet, but he made rather a bony armful and kicked out painfully with his little hooves; also, to tell the truth, he was far from house-trained and his fleece was not as white as snow. My Nannie once washed and dried the rear end of him while the front end was busy with the bottle, much to the farmer's amusement, but it was only a temporary improvement.

If you want to try out these recipes, ask an obliging butcher to supply you with the meat you require. He will probably be surprised but admiring. And do not forget that bone stock, which sets as firm and clear as you could wish, does not necessarily come out of a packet.

It is worth noting that these recipes are often for dishes which will keep for a time, especially potted meats. In the old cool, airy farmhouse larder, most of them kept for a week or more, and this was a great convenience because it meant food was always ready to hand for the hungry, without cooking. And there was, of course, usually a juicy ham 'in cut', ready to carve in thick, pink, glistening slices. I have often been tempted to help myself, in passing, to a slice of ham, rather as children today raid the box of chocolates left lying about. But one staunch farmhouse habit of the shires I have never been able to acquire. The habit of eating great wedges of cold pork or veal and ham pie for Sunday breakfast, all the year round.

Potted meats

The general method for making potted meats and pastes is to cook the meat until soft enough to rub through a sieve, or pound with pestle and mortar. The paste is then highly seasoned and flavoured, pressed into clean, dry pots, and sealed with a layer of clarified butter. If great care is taken they will keep for weeks, even months, until the seal is broken. They can be spread on bread or toast. Potted shrimps are an exception, in that they can be potted whole.

Moulds

These consist of diced meat, poultry or game, sometimes mixed with vegetables, and set in a jelly made from the broth in which they were cooked. A pig's trotter is often added since it gives the broth a high setting quality. Veal bones of any kind are also excellent. The meat is usually packed into moulds which have been rinsed out with cold water, to give a decorative effect round the top and sides, then filled in with the well strained broth, which should set into a bright, clear savoury jelly. Sometimes the broth is considerably reduced or gelatine is added to ensure a perfect set.

Galantines

A galantine is a kind of meat loaf, usually with breadcrumbs and egg to give it sufficient body to be sliced when cold. It can be steamed, boiled, or shaped and baked in the oven. It is usually coated with flavoured and coloured jelly aspic when cold, and sliced from the roll like a joint.

Brawns

Similar to a mould, but the meat and cooking liquor are not always separated, but poured into a basin to set together, so that the jelly is not so clear. Sometimes the meat is pickled before cooking in dry salt, or a wet pickle. A brawn is not considered such a delicate dish as a mould.

To clarify butter: Put the butter in a saucepan, heat it slowly, removing any scum as it forms. When quite clear, pour steadily into clean, dry jars, leaving the sediment behind.

Potted beef

2 LB. LEAN SHIN OF BEEF	GOOD PINCH POWDERED MACE
GOOD PINCH POWDERED CLOVES	SALT AND PEPPER TO TASTE
GOOD PINCH POWDERED	1 TEASPOON ANCHOVY ESSENCE
ALLSPICE	CLARIFIED BUTTER

Trim the meat well, chop finely and put into a stone jar or casserole with 2 tablespoons water, the spices and seasoning. Cover the jar with 2 thicknesses of greasproof paper tied down, and a lid or weighted saucer, and place in a saucepan of boiling water, or in the oven in a roasting tin of boiling water. Simmer gently for 3 hours. Add more boiling water when necessary. Remove the meat, and rub through a sieve. Add a little of the liquid from the meat and the anchovy essence; add more seasoning if necessary. Press the mixture into small pots, and cover with melted clarified butter.

Potted pigeon

3 PIGEONS	PEPPER AND SALT TO TASTE
1 TABLESPOON WORCESTERSHIRE	A LITTLE CLARIFIED BUTTER
SAUCE	

Skin, clean and halve the pigeons. Place them in a saucepan, cover with cold water, bring slowly to the boil, then simmer

147

until tender. Remove from the heat, cool until it is possible to remove all the bones. Mince the meat finely. Re-boil the liquor in the saucepan with the bones and reduce to about ¼ pint. Strain, season with pepper, salt and Worcestershire sauce to taste. Add a little of the stock and a tablespoon of melted butter to the minced meat, and press into small jars. Run sufficient clarified butter over the tops to seal completely.

Potted hare

3 LB. JOINTS OF HARE	½ TEASPOON GRATED NUTMEG
I LB. FAT PORK	I TEASPOON MIXED DRIED
½ TEASPOON PEPPER	SWEET HERBS
SALT TO TASTE	2 OZ. CLARIFIED BUTTER

Bone and mince the hare, and the fat pork. Season with the pepper, herbs, salt and nutmeg and mince again. Pound with a pestle and mortar or the end of a wooden rolling pin in a bowl, until it resembles a fine paste. Turn into an earthenware pot, cover with a flour and water paste crust. Bake in a moderate oven for 2 hours. Have ready the clarified butter, remove the crust and pour a good layer of butter over the surface while it is still hot.

Chicken paste

I CHICKEN, OR BOILING FOWL	I PEELED ONION
6 OZ. BUTTER	I DESSERTSPOON
I LEVEL TEASPOON SUGAR	WORCESTERSHIRE SAUCE
½ TEASPOON PEPPERCORNS	GOOD PINCH CAYENNE PEPPER
½ TEASPOON ALLSPICE	CLARIFIED BUTTER
½ TEASPOON CLOVES	

Clean the chicken, cut into joints, put into a casserole with the butter, sugar, peeled onion, and the whole spices tied in a muslin bag. Cover closely, if necessary using a strip of flour and water paste to seal the lid. Cook in a slow oven for 3 hours or until the meat is tender. Cool, strip meat from the bones, discard the spices, and put the meat through the fine blade of the mincer. Pound well together with the rest of the butter, sauce, cayenne pepper and, if liked, another pinch of sugar. Press into small pots and cover with clarified butter.

Many farms are close to the sea, and so it is not unusual to find fish or shellfish on the farmhouse menu. However, as they were not often available, treats like shrimps used sometimes to be preserved in the form of paste, or potted like this.

Potted shrimps: Peel 2 pints of cooked shrimps while they are still warm (or plunge into boiling water for 1 minute before shelling) and stir in 3 oz. melted butter, a grating of nutmeg and a shake of pepper. Press into small pots, and cover with clarified butter.

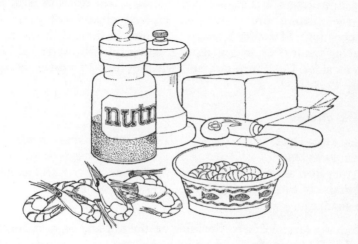

Shrimp paste

1 PINT SHRIMPS	PINCH CAYENNE PEPPER
8 OZ. FRESH HADDOCK OR	PINCH POWDERED MACE
HAKE	BUTTER
FEW DROPS ANCHOVY SAUCE	CLARIFIED BUTTER

Carefully flake the fish. Cook the shrimps, drain, reserving the water in which they were boiled. Shell them and cook the flaked fish in the shrimp water until soft. Allow to cool, and pound to a smooth paste with the spices and anchovy sauce. Measure the quantity and beat in an equal amount of butter. Gradually beat in the whole shrimps. Heat the mixture until hot, but not bubbling, and turn into small pots. Cover well with clarified butter and cool quickly.

Beef galantine

I LB. STEWING STEAK	2 OZ. SOFT WHITE
6 OZ. STREAKY BACON	BREADCRUMBS
8 OZ. BEEF SAUSAGE MEAT	2 EGGS
SALT AND PEPPER TO TASTE	LITTLE BEEF STOCK
GOOD PINCH DRIED HERBS	½ PINT ASPIC JELLY

Put the beef and bacon together through the mincer, using a fine blade, then bind together with all the other ingredients except the aspic, and add only sufficient stock to give a mixture you can form into a loaf shape. Well grease a loaf tin with lard, put in the mixture and cover with greased greaseproof paper (or kitchen foil). Steam for 2 hours. This may be done in the oven, by placing the loaf tin in a shallow roasting tin with water half way up its sides. Cool, turn out, and when quite cold, coat with aspic jelly. Serve in slices.

Pork cheese

I LB. LEAN PORK	I TABLESPOON FRESH HERBS,
I LB. FAT PORK	FINELY CHOPPED (SUCH AS
2 TEASPOONS SALT	PARSLEY, THYME AND SAGE)
½ TEASPOON WHITE PEPPER	½ PINT ASPIC JELLY
12 SHALLOTS	

Chop the meat coarsely. Sprinkle on the salt and pepper, and the herbs. Peel and finely chop the shallots; or chives or spring onions may be used instead, according to the season. Press the mixture into a Yorkshire pudding tin, and bake in a moderate oven for I hour. Allow to cool slightly, then pour over the aspic jelly stock. Put aside to set, and serve scooped out or cut in slices. This goes well with crisp green salad.

Granny Turpin's mould

I COW'S HEEL	2 LARGE CARROTS
I LB. SHIN OF BEEF	I LB. GREEN PEAS
4 OZ. COOKED HAM	SALT AND PEPPER TO TASTE

Dice the beef and ham, and put in a saucepan with the cow's heel. Just cover with water, season to taste, and cover. Simmer for 2 hours. Peel and dice the carrots, shell the peas, add the vege-

tables and cook for a further $\frac{1}{2}$ hour. When the meat and vegetables are tender, cool the cow's heel and strip off the meat, and
dice it. Arrange the diced meat and vegetables in a large mould
that has been rinsed with cold water, then strain the cooking
liquid over it. Turn out when set.

Note: This is a good supper dish, especially if a few shelled
hard-boiled eggs are quartered and served as a garnish.

Sheep's head mould

1 SHEEP'S HEAD	1 BAY LEAF
1 PIG'S TROTTER	A BOUQUET GARNI
1 LB. ONIONS	SALT AND PEPPER TO TASTE
1 LB. CARROTS	1 LB. PARSNIPS
1 STICK CELERY	2 OZ. BARLEY
2 CLOVES	

Have the butcher split the head and remove eyes, offal and brain.
Wash in cold water, then put in a saucepan with peeled parsnips, 2
peeled onions, 2 peeled carrots, the green parts of the celery,
the herbs, spices and seasoning. Cover with cold water, and
bring to the boil, skim carefully. Cover and simmer for 2 hours.
Sieve the meat and vegetables, reserving the liquid. Remove the
bones, bring the liquid to the boil again. Add the barley and
the rest of the carrots, onions and celery, nicely prepared and
diced, and cook until tender. Meanwhile dice up all the meat
from the head and trotter, and add to the pan. Arrange the
meat and vegetables round the sides of a large mould, or two
smaller ones, put the barley in the middle. Boil the stock until
it is thick, and there is only enough left to fill the moulds. Pour
in gently, and leave to set. There will be quite a thick film of fat
on top, but do not remove this. Turn out and serve with salad.

Note: If no pig's trotter is available, add a little gelatine to the
reduced broth to ensure a set.

Poacher's rabbit brawn

1 LARGE RABBIT	SALT AND PEPPER TO TASTE
2 PIG'S TROTTERS	GOOD PINCH ALLSPICE

Put the pig's feet in a large saucepan with sufficient cold water
to cover, and simmer gently for $1\frac{1}{2}$ hours. Meanwhile skin, clean

151

and joint the rabbit, and soak in salt water for ½ hour. Drain, and add to the saucepan. Bring to the boil again, and simmer for another 2 hours or until the rabbit flesh is tender. Remove from the heat, cool until it is possible to remove all the bones. Chop the meat finely, season with the salt, pepper and spice, return to the saucepan. Bring to the boil again, then pour into 2 pudding basins, rinsed out with cold water. Allow to stand until well set, turn out and serve with salad.

Note: Since rabbit is now becoming scarce in some parts of the country this recipe is excellent made with imported rabbit. In the old days, a poacher could put the trotters on to cook, go out and find a rabbit in one of his snares and have it ready to add to the pot just when needed.

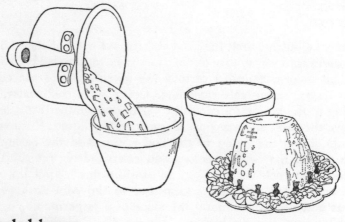

Dappled brawn

½ PIG'S HEAD	I LARGE ONION, PEELED
FEW PEPPERCORNS	SALT AND PEPPER TO TASTE
I BOILING FOWL	I LARGE SPRIG PARSLEY

Cover the ½ pig's head in salt, leave for 3 days. Then soak for 2 hours in fresh water, and scrub off all the salt. Put in a large saucepan with the peppercorns and simmer until tender. Cool, and remove all rough pieces of skin, and skin the tongue. Chop coarsely. Meanwhile, clean and joint the fowl, put in a saucepan together with the giblets in just enough water to cover. Add salt and pepper to taste, the onion and the parsley sprig. Cover and simmer until tender. Cool, remove all the bones and cut up the flesh. Reserve the white meat for the bottom and sides of the moulds. Pack 2 or 3 large moulds with the meat, using alternate layers of pork and chicken. Mix the 2 cooking liquors, boil up and reduce a little, strain and season to taste with salt and pepper. Pour into the moulds, and allow to set. If correctly arranged, the outer surface of the moulds will show dappled layers of pink and white meat when turned out.

Pig's head brawn

1 PIG'S HEAD	2 TABLESPOONS DRIED SAGE
2 PIG'S TROTTERS	SALT AND PEPPER TO TASTE
2 LB. ONIONS	CRUSHED SALT

You really need a very large saucepan or boiler for this brawn. Have the pig's head split, the eyes, offal and brains removed. Rub the pieces and the trotters with crushed salt, and arrange closely in a large basin. Sprinkle with more salt. Leave for 2 days. Wash well in cold water, and place in a large saucepan. Cover with water. Bring to the boil, skim well, and simmer gently for about 3 hours or until the meat is tender. Remove the pork pieces on to an enamel tray, remove all the meat. Mince it, along with the peeled onions. Season with dried sage and pepper and add salt to taste. Remove as much fat as possible from the liquor. Strain it, then put a measured 4 quarts of the liquor into the saucepan and add all the meat mixture. Simmer for 20 minutes, stirring from time to time. Pour into a number of moulds and basins. Turn out when cold and well set.

To make a raised pie: For a pie sufficiently large to serve 4–6 you will need for the hot-water pastry crust:

12 OZ. PLAIN FLOUR	$\frac{1}{4}$ PINT WARM WATER
GOOD PINCH SALT	EGG FOR GLAZING
4 OZ. LARD (SLIGHTLY WARM)	

Sieve the flour and salt into a basin and rub in 1 oz. of the lard. Melt the rest of the fat in the warm water, and add to the flour. Mix with a knife blade until it forms lumps, then knead quickly with the hands. You must work rapidly as the pastry should still be warm when moulded. Set aside one third of the pastry (covered with a warm cloth) for the pie-lid. Roll out the remaining dough, put a 2 lb. jam jar in the centre and mould the pastry up round this to make a pie about 6 inches deep. Turn on its side and roll it to and fro to make the sides smooth. (An expert cook can mould the pastry round her own fist without using a mould, but some farmhouses still possess solid wooden moulds for the purpose.) Put in the filling as soon as the mould is withdrawn, turn the top edge of the pastry in over it, damp the edge and cover with the lid. Press edges together firmly, and makes cuts at $\frac{1}{2}$ inch intervals round the top to secure.

Note: Rather more rare than wooden moulds are metal hinged pie cases in very fancy designs, which fit round the pie during baking and are removed for the last few minutes of baking, to brown the sides. These give fancy oval or diamond shapes to the pie. A very old hinged case was used for the veal and ham pie shown in the colour photograph on the front of this book.

Melton Mowbray pie

HOT-WATER PIE CRUST MADE
    FROM 12 OZ. FLOUR
$1\frac{1}{2}$ LB. LEAN PORK
4 OZ. FAT PORK
SALT AND PEPPER TO TASTE

6 ANCHOVY FILLETS OR I
    TEASPOON ANCHOVY ESSENCE
$\frac{1}{2}$ TEASPOON DRIED SAGE
ABOUT $\frac{1}{4}$ PINT VEAL STOCK

Make the pie crust as directed, and prepare the case. Dice the meat, blend with the pounded achovies or essence, add the sage and seasoning, but not too much salt, as anchovies are salt. Fill the case and cover. Bake and finish as for veal and ham pie.

Note: The anchovies give the meat the delicate flavour and pink colour always associated with pies from Melton Mowbray.

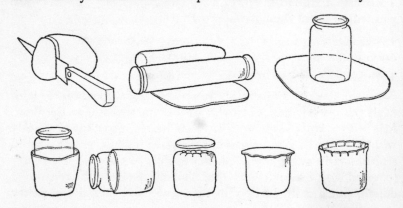

Veal and ham pie

HOT WATER CRUST PASTRY
    MADE WITH 12 OZ. FLOUR
1¼ LB. FILLET OF VEAL
6 OZ. HAM, IN ONE SLICE
2 HARD-BOILED EGGS,
    SHELLED

SMALL PINCH GROUND GINGER
SMALL PINCH GROUND NUTMEG
½ LEVEL TEASPOON GRATED
    LEMON RIND
SALT AND PEPPER TO TASTE
ABOUT ¼ PINT VEAL STOCK

Reserve one third of the pastry for the lid, and use the rest to line a greased 1 lb. loaf tin. Trim and dice both meats into small cubes. Mix with the salt, pepper and grated lemon rind. Place half the meat in the bottom of the tin, arrange the eggs lengthwise on top, and press the rest of the meat firmly round and over them. Sprinkle about 3 tablespoons of veal stock over it. Turn the top of the pastry in all round. Roll out the remaining one third of pastry to form the lid, damp the edges, press on top, pinch the edges together. Make a hole in the centre, brush over with beaten egg and decorate with pastry leaves cut from the trimmings, then brush over again. Bake in the centre of a moderate oven, reducing the heat slightly after the first hour, for 2–2½ hours. Immediately pour in sufficient veal stock through the centre hole to fill the pie. Remove from the tin when completely cold, and the jelly is set. *Note :* If the stock is not strong enough to set into a firm jelly, dissolve ½ teaspoon powdered gelatine in the warm stock, but make sure the gelatine is fully dissolved, and pour in while still syrupy.

Collared beef

6 LB. PIECE BEEF FLANK
2 OZ. SOFT BROWN SUGAR
6 OZ. SALT
1 OZ. SALTPETRE
1 DESSERTSPOON DRIED SAGE

LARGE BUNCH FRESH MIXED
    HERBS
½ TEASPOON POWDERED
    ALLSPICE
SALT AND PEPPER TO TASTE

Put the piece of beef into a dish, rub in salt, saltpetre and sugar. Leave in a cool larder for 7 days, turning and rubbing the meat every day. Bone and trim the meat of gristle, wash it well. Sprinkle with the herbs, spice and seasoning, roll up in a boiling cloth and tie tightly. Put the bones in a large saucepan with sufficient water to cover, the joint and, if liked, a few pot vegetables. Simmer the meat gently for 5 hours. Remove from the boiling bag, and press under a weight until cold and set.

Appendix

The art of home freezing

Farmers' wives have long been the pioneers of preserving food by freezing it at home. Although this is the least venerable of the domestic arts it is coming to rank high on the list of a country housewife's accomplishments.

It is cheaper, quicker and easier to freeze down a glut of garden or orchard produce than to bottle or can it. When the calendar has moved forward a few months, the juicy fruit or tender vegetables taken for granted during their season become quite a delicacy; often one which costs nothing but the packing materials in the first place. On a farm there is always the possibility of being presented with a whole carcass of an animal, or several brace of game birds, which cannot be used up immediately. A really large chest freezer (for the farmhouse kitchen usually has room for one of these super-sized economizers, so far exempt from tax) finds space for it all, and once frozen the food is safe for many months.

Freezing is the most natural of all forms of food preservation. It works quite simply, by reducing the temperature of food below the level at which bacteria are active; they become dormant, thus preventing any further deterioration. Not destroyed, merely *dormant*; which means that the food must be extremely clean and fresh, and handled under the most hygienic conditions when prepared for freezing. Then the thawing process which again raises the temperature to the zone of bacterial activity will not wake a host of slumbering bacteria at the same time!

Rules for safe freezing

Certain rules must be followed to prepare food for freezing, protect it while in the freezer, and eventually thaw it out in good condition.

1. Choose only food for freezing which is in perfect, peak condition. Freezing does not improve the quality, merely preserves it.
2. Prepare for freezing as soon as possible after picking, slaughtering or (in the case of cooked foods) cooking. This arrests deterioration at the earliest possible stage.
3. Keep the food itself, your hands, any implements used, and the packing materials perfectly clean. This prevents unnecessary

further contamination. For the same reason, cool all cooked foods quickly.

4. Blanch all vegetables, and cool quickly. Vegetables, unlike fruit, are a non-acidic food, and require this extra precaution to halt enzyme activity which continues even after freezing.

5. Pack food with an airtight seal in moisture-vapour-proof materials. Those suitable include polythene containers with snap-on lids, guaranteed not to split or warp at sub-zero temperatures, such as Tupperware, heavy gauge polythene bags, waxed cartons, heavy duty foil and sheet polythene. The cold, dry air of the freezer must be prevented from entering the pack, absorbing moisture from the food and causing dehydration. Equally, the moisture in the food must not be drawn out through the pack into the dry air of the cabinet.

6. Eliminate airspaces, other than necessary headspaces to allow for the expansion of the water content of the food on freezing. Airspaces allow moisture to be drawn out of the food to cause frost formation inside the packs. Here are two safe ways to wrap food.

Butcher's wrap: Take a square sheet of polythene, each side a little longer than the object to be wrapped. Place the food diagonally across one corner, turn the corner over and tuck it firmly under the food, then roll forward, bringing the corners which stick out at either side into the middle. Fold in tightly, and continue rolling, making sure the folded wrapping narrows towards the opposite corner. Fix the point securely with freezer tape.

Druggist's wrap: Place the food to be wrapped in the centre of a rectangle of polythene, large enough for the usual type of parcel.

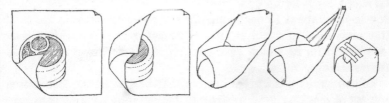

Bring the opposite long sides together across the top, fold over and over to enclose the object tightly. Fasten with polytape to secure while the ends are folded in. Fold one end to a point, bring over and secure at the centre, then the other end.

7. Seal with freezer tape (ordinary sealing tapes crack at low temperatures) or use twist ties. Label with self-adhesive labels

and chinagraph or crayon pencil, stating contents and date frozen.

8. Freeze down fast, as soon as the food is completely cold. Slow freezing allows more time for ice crystals to form in the food cells, as it passes through the temperature zone at which water freezes. These crystals pierce the cell walls and do irreparable damage, causing the texture to be flabby when the food is defrosted. Put the packs into the fast-freeze compartment, lower the temperature dial or throw the fast-freeze switch, according to your type of freezer. Restore to normal (between 0°F. and −5°F.) when food is fully frozen.

9. Keep fully frozen until required. Do not allow to partially defrost then put back in the freezer. Defrost according to these rules:

Meat and poultry: Slowly, if possible in the refrigerator for several hours or overnight according to the size and density of the pack. Large joints and whole birds take longest.

Vegetables: These need not be thawed, and should be cooked from the frozen state, except corn on the cob, which needs thawing first. They take only a short time, having been partly cooked by blanching.

Fruit: To be served uncooked, allow to thaw slowly and serve slightly chilled. Allow 4–6 hours at room temperature, 6–8 hours in the refrigerator. Fruit for cooking should be partially thawed first.

Baked goods: Unwrap cakes while still frozen to prevent damage to decorations, thaw at room temperature 1–3 hours according to size. Bread should be thawed in the same way. Frozen bread may be sliced for toasting or frying.

Made-up dishes: Reheat gently in a covered casserole in the oven (for pies bake in a hot oven); or reheat over gentle direct heat in a saucepan, in which case stir frequently to prevent the food from sticking.

Of course there is a great deal more to be said on the fascinating subject of stocking a home freezer, taking into account commercially as well as home-freezing food, and there are now many excellent books on the subject. But it is a pleasant thought that farmhouse cookery, always typifying the best of our British traditional cuisine, has continued to lead the way in this, the latest and most advanced method of preserving and presenting food for the family table.

Index

angelica, preserved, 142

bacon, pickled, 88
barm brack, 132
Bath chaps, pickled, 86
beans, salting, 83
beef: collared, 155; galantine, 150;
   pickled, 84–5; potted, 147
beer-making, 29–32; basic, 30–1;
   ginger, 31; nettle, 32
beestings, 109
beestings custard, 109
bottling: fruit, 66–71; vegetables,
   71–3, 74
brandy, apricot, 120
brawns, 147, 151–3; dappled, 152–3;
   pig's head, 153; poacher's rabbit,
   151–2
bread-making, 121–7; baking
   powder, 127; baps, 126–7;
   cottage loaf, 123; flower pot
   loaves, 125; harvest loaf, 123–4;
   malt loaf, 124; quick wheatmeal,
   125; Wiltshire lardy cake, 126;
   white, 122–3
buns, Yorkshire tea, 130
butter-making, 112, 113–14;
   apple, 113; grape, 113–14;
   quince, 114
butterscotch, 135

candied peel, 142
candy, pulled, 137
canning: fruit, 75–6; vegetables, 75,
   76
cheese-making, 99–107, 112–13,
   114–15; apple and mint, 115;
   apple and sage, 115; Banffshire
   'picking', 103; blackberry, 114;
   buttermilk crowdie, 107;
   Cheddar-type, 102–3; cottage,
   107; cream, 106; farmhouse
   gorgonzola, 105; caraway seed,
   105; damson, 115; medlar, 115;
   Shropshire sage, 104–5;
   Wensleydale, 103–4
cheese-cakes from curds, 108
chicken paste, 148
chutney-making, 51–4, 58–61;
   apple and tomato, 60; gooseberry,
   61; green tomato, 58; marrow,
   60–1; orange, 61; plum, 59;
   plum and apple, 60; rhubarb,
   58–9; turnip, 59
cider-making, 28–9
coconut ice, 139

cooking: dried fruits, 93; dried
   vegetables, 95; salt beef or pork,
   86; salted ox tongue, 85–6
cream, clotted, 100, 107–8
crumpets, 131
curds: fruit, 115; lemon, 116;
   marrow, 116; and whey, 108
curing, 77–81; Derbyshire, 80–1;
   Devonshire, 80; Leicestershire,
   81; Yorkshire, 80

drinks made from milk and cream:
   Hampshire posset, 110; hatted
   kit, 110; milk punch, 110;
   orange syllabub, 110; rich
   syllabub, 109
drying: fruit, 92–3; herbs, 95–8;
   vegetables, 93–5

egg preserving, 89–90

fish, smoked, 87
flowers, crystallized, 143–4
fondants, fruit, 140–1
freezing, 156–8
fudge: honey, 136; treacle nut, 136

galantines, 146–7, 150
gin: blackcurrant, 120; sloe, 120
grapes and oranges, crystallized, 144

ham: baking, 81; boiling, 81–2;
   curing, 77–81; finishing, 82–3;
   smoking, 77–8, 79, 80, 81;
   storing, 79, 81
hare, potted, 148
herbs, 95–8
herrings: pickled, 87; salting, 86–7
humbugs, mint, 136

jam-making, 33–43, 48–9; apple
   ginger, 41; apricot, 40; chestnut,
   42; fig and lemon, 36–7; gooseberry and strawberry, 42–3; green
   tomato and apple, 38
   hedgerow, 41; huckleberry, 37;
   japonica, 37; melon and lemon,
   42; Morello cherry, 39; rhubarb
   and ginger, 40–1; rose hip and
   apple, 42; rose petal, 38; plum,
   37–8; raspberry, 38–9;
   strawberry, 40

jelly-making, 43–7, 48–9, 138;
   apple geranium, 45; bramble,